Fourth Edition

The Skipper's Pocketbook

A pocket database for the busy skipper

Updated by Sara Hopkinson
Originally compiled by Basil Mosenthal

www.fernhurstbooks.com

Fourth edition published by Fernhurst Books Limited in 2025 – Print 1

The Windmill, Mill Lane, Harbury, Leamington Spa, Warwickshire. CV33 9HP. UK. www.fernhurstbooks.com
Tel: +44 (0) 1926 337488 | fernhurst@fernhurstbooks.com

EU GPSR Authorised Representative:
LOGOS EUROPE, 9 rue Nicolas Poussin, 17000, LA ROCHELLE, France
E-mail: Contact@logoseurope.eu

Third edition published by Fernhurst Books Limited in 2018
Second edition published by Fernhurst Books in 2001
First edition published by Fernhurst Books in 1999

A catalogue record for this book is available from the British Library
ISBN 978-1-917801-02-7

All photographs © Fernhurst Books Limited
Except: Crewsaver p1, 9, 10 (top), 11, 16; EP Barrus p85, 87; ICOM p12; Nasa Marine p65; Raymarine p1, 24, 38; Seasafe p20 (bottom).

Designed & typeset by Daniel Stephen
Printed in India by Manipal Technologies Limited

CONTENTS

INTRODUCTION

It is easy to take for granted how much a skipper needs to know.

Navigation, how to pilot the boat into a new harbour, using the radio, checking the engine, keeping an eye out for things that need repair, monitoring the weather, feeding the crew and much, much more!

This pocketbook is designed as a pocket database, with checklists to make life easier for busy skippers.

Fernhurst Books also recommend it as an invaluable reference book for the RYA® Yachtmaster® syllabus.

I have been delighted to be able to thoroughly update this fourth edition of this great book which has been in publication since 1999.

With this book in your pocket, I hope you will have many happy hours afloat.

Sara Hopkinson

Sara Hopkinson is an experienced sailor, a Yachtmaster ® Instructor and Examiner and lives at Pin Mill in Suffolk where she runs an RYA ® Training Centre which specialises in navigation, radio, radar and first aid courses. She was a Coastguard Rescue Officer for many years and Station Officer of HM Coastguard Holbrook. Sara has written books for the RYA ® and Fernhurst Books' *Navigation: A Newcomer's Guide*, *VHF Afloat* and *VHF Companion*.

Basil Mosenthal sailed extensively in all the oceans of the world. After leaving the Royal Navy he was partner in one of the first yacht delivery firms. He has written many books about sailing, including Fernhurst Books' best-selling *Cockpit Companion* and *New Crew's Companion*.

This book also incorporates material by Tim Davison, David Houghton & Pat Manley.

Additional Rescources
Scan the QR code or visit www.fernhurstbooks.com, search for Skipper's Pocketbook and click on 'Additional Rescources'

PART 1.
PREPARING FOR SEA

CHECKLIST: PREPARING FOR SEA

- ☐ Weather forecast
- ☐ Engine checks
- ☐ Fuel level
- ☐ Safety equipment in place
- ☐ VHF radio & instruments on
- ☐ Passage planned, including route, waypoints, tidal heights, location of hazards & a contingency plan
- ☐ Chart plotter, GNSS & charts
- ☐ Crew briefed on safety equipment & passage
- ☐ Compass & navigation lights tested
- ☐ All gear stowed
- ☐ Food prepared & galley tidy
- ☐ All hatches shut
- ☐ Bilges dry
- ☐ Mainsail reefing set up
- ☐ Sail cover off & sails ready to go
- ☐ Radar reflector in position
- ☐ Information about passage left ashore
- ☐ RYA SafeTrx App updated for passage
- ☐ Water full
- ☐ Rubbish ashore
- ☐ Gas
- ☐ Crew ready, waterproofs, boots, lifejackets
- ☐ Anchor ready, with no gear stored on top in case it is needed in a hurry
- ☐ ____________________
- ☐ ____________________
- ☐ ____________________
- ☐ ____________________
- ☐ ____________________
- ☐ ____________________
- ☐ ____________________

Download from www.fernhurstbooks.com, search for Skipper's Pocketbook and click on 'Additional Rescources'

CHECKLIST: SAFETY ITEMS

Gas

- ☐ Store cylinders upright in a locker that drains overboard
- ☐ Have system professionally inspected
- ☐ Fit an audible alarm with sensor below cooker or in bilge
- ☐ Turn off gas at cylinder when not in use

Galley

- ☐ Lock gimbals when not at sea
- ☐ Fit crash bar to prevent the cook falling onto the stove
- ☐ Cook must wear protection on legs & feet in rough weather
- ☐ Provide galley strap

Outboards

- ☐ Store on deck, on the pushpit
- ☐ Spare fuel carried on deck, or in a locker that vents overboard

The dinghy

- ☐ Don't overload with too many people & kit, & load evenly
- ☐ Wear lifejackets
- ☐ Consider carrying oars, spare fuel, torch, small anchor, portable VHF or mobile phone & pump
- ☐ Climb in & out with care, & do not use when drunk

Clothing

- ☐ Warm, waterproof clothing
- ☐ Non-slip shoes & boots
- ☐ Polarised sunglasses & hat

Deck

- ☐ Control mainsheet when gybing
- ☐ Fit non-slip treads to hatches
- ☐ Provide jackstays
- ☐ Use a preventer when running

Download from www.fernhurstbooks.com, search for Skipper's Pocketbook and click on 'Additional Rescources'

CHECKLIST: SAFETY BRIEFING

Brief the crew on:

- ☐ Use of lifejackets, safety lines & jackstays when clipping on
- ☐ MOB procedure, including use of equipment
- ☐ How to start the engine
- ☐ Use of the cooker, including gas safety
- ☐ Location & use of fire blanket & extinguishers
- ☐ How to fire extinguisher into engine space, if there is not an automatic system
- ☐ How to use the radio & send a Distress Alert & Mayday
- ☐ Location & operating procedure for flares & EPIRB
- ☐ How to launch the liferaft
- ☐ Location of first aid kit
- ☐ Safe areas to sit, away from the mainsheet & boom, in the case of an accidental gybe

Download from www.fernhurstbooks.com, search for Skipper's Pocketbook and click on 'Additional Rescources'

It is useful to have a few lockers labelled or a plan of the boat or a list showing the storage of the safety equipment, and to have a few notes or photographs to remind crew of the safety brief information.

Item	Location

PART 2. SAFETY EQUIPMENT & PROCEDURES

SAFETY EQUIPMENT

All equipment must be:

- in-date
- professionally serviced
- in position
- understood by all on board

Lifejackets

Wearing a lifejacket is the normal thing to do, unless the skipper has decided that it is safe not to.

They should be a minimum of 150 Newtons, be fitted with a crotch strap or thigh straps and be adjusted to fit snugly. Additionally, at extra cost, they can:

- be automatic
- have a safety line attachment point
- be fitted with a light, a MOB beacon / personal AIS transponder, or PLB
- include a sprayhood

Jackets should be checked regularly to ensure:

- the bottle is not corroded and is screwed in tightly
- the firing head on an automatic lifejacket has not expired
- the light is in date

Lifejacket

Safety line attachment

Inflated lifejacket with hood

Children need their own lifejackets with a crotch strap, which fit correctly. Too large is dangerous as the child will not be supported high enough in the water. Auto-inflate lifejackets are also available for children from about 6 or 8.

Safety harnesses & safety lines

Safety harnesses are generally integral with lifejackets and attachment points must be available near the main companion-way. Ideally, there should be jackstays down each sidedeck to clip onto when moving about the boat.

Clipping on is recommended at night and in heavy weather.

Personal location devices

Small units designed to be worn inside a lifejacket. **Personal location devices have licensing and regulation requirements.**

PLB, Person Location Beacon: Once activated sends a signal to the Coastguard via satellite, in a similar way to an EPIRB.

MOB beacon / Personal AIS transponder: These activate when the lifejacket inflates, sending a local AIS signal alerting the boat and placing a new waypoint on the chart plotter, which updates for drift via built-in GNSS.

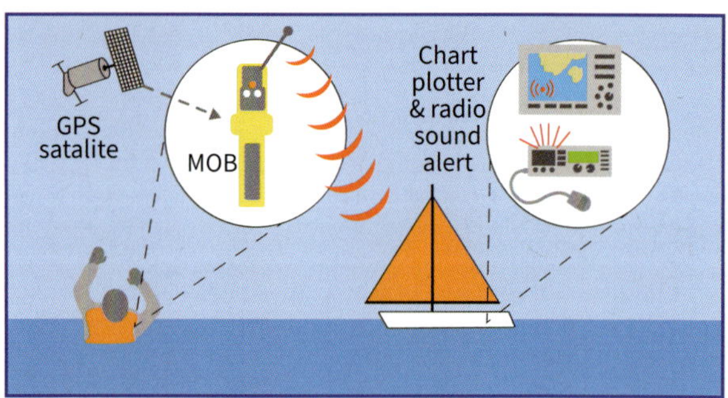

New technology develops rapidly so getting the latest expert advice is important.

Radar reflector

A good quality radar reflector is essential for a GRP or wooden boat, permanently mounted at a height of at least 4 metres.

The most effective are the large white reflectors.

The boat may also have AIS or an Active Radar Target Enchancer, but both are dependent on the vesssel's power supply, so a passive reflector is still required.

Other equipment

- **Bilge pumps:** Ideally have 2, one operated in the cockpit and one below, at least one should be manual. Each should have a strum box or strainer fitted. Carry buckets as well.
- **Softwood bungs:** Attach to each through-hull fitting.
- **Rope cutter:** A rope or net around the propeller shaft will stop the engine, and may damage the stern gland or gearbox. Fit a rope cutter on the shaft.
- **Emergency tiller** on a wheel-steered boat. Try it out to ensure that it fits and learn how it works.
- **Searchlight** and torches.

MAN OVERBOARD (MOB)

MOB equipment

Lifebelt, with drogue and light, marked with vessel's name.

Equipment

- Two horseshoe lifebelt, or one plus a lifesling
- Each lifebelt should have a drogue
- One lifebelt should have a buoyant light
- A dan-buoy should be attached to one lifebelt
- A buoyant heaving line should be within reach of the helmsman
- A tackle system for recovering the MOB
- A boarding ladder, long enough for the person in the water to climb onto

MOB procedures

If someone falls overboard:

- Shout "man overboard"
- Press the MOB button on the chart plotter, it will show the position as a new waypoint & suspend the current route
- Appoint a look-out
- Throw MOB equipment
- Send a Distress Alert and Mayday

Methods for returning to the casualty

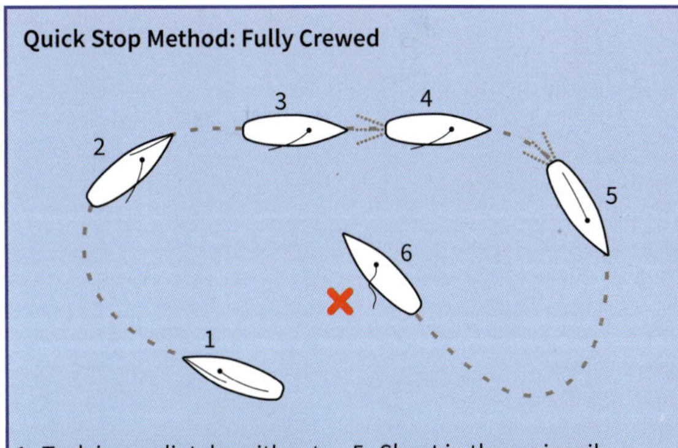

1. Tack immediately, without touching the sheets.
2. The boat will heave to.
3. Furl the jib.
4. Check for ropes. Start the engine.
5. Sheet in the mainsail. If the engine fails, sail through step 5 and approach MOB on a close reach.
6. Pick up on leeward side. Use the engine to assist if necessary.

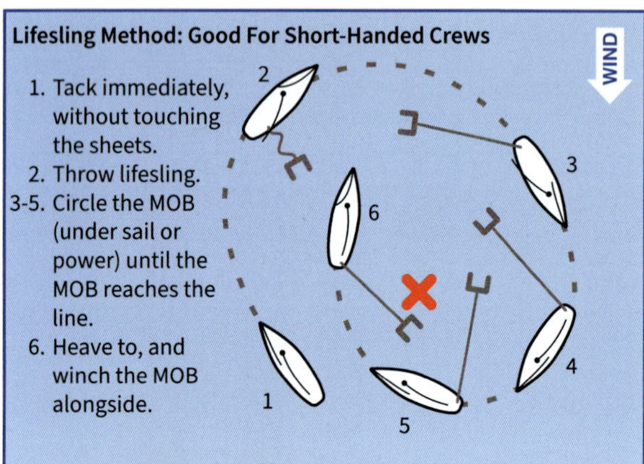

Lifesling

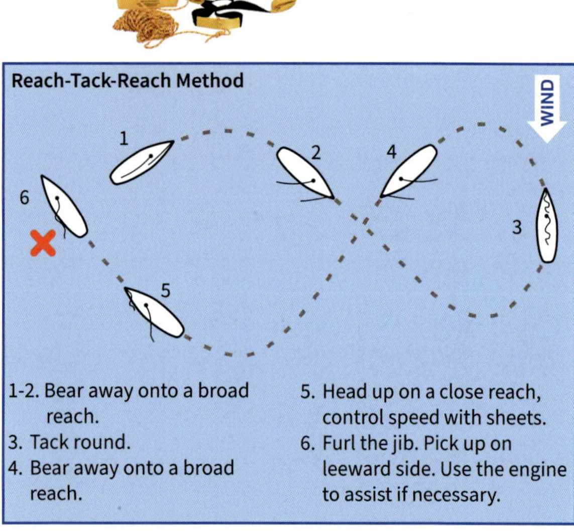

VHF RADIO

Modern VHF/DSC radios make both routine calling and distress communications easier and more effective. For routine DSC calls it is convenient to save frequently used MMSI numbers into the contacts list, as on a mobile phone.

It is important that the correct channel is used, and the minimum power setting, to avoid interference. For routine calling, such as to marinas and other boats, use 1 watt.

Radio channels

International distress channel (essential calling only)	Ch 16
DSC channel (not to be used for voice)	Ch 70
Inter-ship channels	Ch 06, 08,72,77
Bridge to bridge on matters of navigational safety	Ch 13
Channel used by HM Coastguard to communicate with small craft	Ch 67
Coastguard MSI broadcasts	Ch 62, 63, 64
Port operations	Check in almanac
UK marinas	Ch 80
NCI channel	Ch 65
Race control / safety boats	Ch M (37) / M2

DISTRESS SIGNALS

Internationally recognised distress signals

Continuous sounding of the fog horn	Hand-held red flare, or parachute rocket
Orange smoke signal	Morse code SOS sent by light or sound ●●● ▬ ▬ ▬ ●●●
The spoken word MAYDAY	Slowly & repeated raising & lowering outstretched arms
Distress Alert on VHF/DSC radio	An EPIRB
International code flags N over C	A square flag above or below a ball, or anything resembling a ball
Gun or explosive signal fired at intervals of about 1 minute	Flames on the foredeck as from a burning barrel of tar

- Any sighting of a visual distress signal MUST be reported to the Coastguard.
- Using a distress signal when not in distress is ILLEGAL, as well as irresponsible (e.g. setting off flares and rockets on Bonfire Night).
- Time-expired flares should be disposed of legally and safely.

Monitoring bodies

HM Coastguard co-ordinate all civilian search and rescue at sea and along the coast of the UK. They call upon one or more of the 350 Coastguard Rescue Teams round the coast, Coastguard helicopters and other resources such as the RNLI and independent lifeboats. Coastguard Rescue Teams are trained in search, first aid, water, mud and rope rescue and are on call 24 hours.

In an emergency send a DSC Distress Alert, followed by a Mayday, and for routine matters use an individual DSC call using the MMSI of the nearest full-time station to contact the Coastguard. The MMSI number will be found in the almanac.

The Coastguard also make regular Maritime Safety Information broadcasts with navigation warnings and weather forecasts. Times and details are in the almanac.

The **NCI** (National Coastwatch Instituition) keep a visual and listening watch at various locations around the coast, and can be contacted by VHF on Channel 65 for radio checks, weather forecasts and other local information. Details of locations and times of watch keeping are on their website.

To find out more scan the QR code or visit www.nci.org.uk/stations

Other counties have similar organisations (e.g. US Coast Guard – www.uscg.mil)

RYA SafeTrx

This free App allows HM Coastguard to access information about the vessel in an emergency and has many other useful features.

Radio distress procedure

Mayday

Should only be used in the case of grave and imminent danger to a person, vessel, vehicle or aircraft.

Have a Mayday procedure card available by the radio, with the vessel name, call sign and MMSI written in. Before the spoken Mayday it is important to send a DSC Distress Alert. The Alert will include the vessel ID and position, and will be received by all DSC sets within range.

To send a DSC DISTRESS ALERT

Lift the red cover, then press and hold the distress button until the alert is sent.

To send a MAYDAY
Transmit voice Mayday on Channel 16 on high power.

MAYDAY, MAYDAY, MAYDAY
This is – *boat name spoken three times*
Call sign and MMSI

MAYDAY – *boat name once*
Callsign and MMSI
My position is ... *give latitude and longitude or range and bearing from a known point*
Nature of distress: *sinking, fire, MOB*
I require immediate assistance
Number of people on board
Any other information: *type of vessel, abandoning to liferaft, no liferaft*
Over

A mobile phone is not a substitute for a VHF radio in an emergency – it can only be heard by one person, the signal may be lost, the battery may go flat and any position obtained is far less accurate. But, if there is nothing else, dial 999 and ask for the Coastguard.

Pan Pan

A Pan Pan message can be used if the situation is urgent, but not life-threatening. It can be preceded by an Urgency Announcement on DSC.

To send a PAN PAN
Use Channel 16 on high power.

PAN PAN, PAN PAN, PAN PAN
All stations – All stations – All stations
This is – *boat name spoken three times*
MMSI
My position is ... *give latitude and longitude or range and bearing from a known point*
Nature of problem
Assistance required
Over

In case of dismasting, a spare antenna that can be fitted at deck level or a portable VHF are useful.

Phonetic alphabet

A	ALPHA	J	JULIET	S	SIERRA
B	BRAVO	K	KILO	T	TANGO
C	CHARLIE	L	LIMA	U	UNIFORM
D	DELTA	M	MIKE	V	VICTOR
E	ECHO	N	NOVEMBER	W	WHISKY
F	FOXTROT	O	OSCAR	X	X-RAY
G	GOLF	P	PAPA	Y	YANKEE
H	HOTEL	Q	QUEBEC	Z	ZULU
I	INDIA	R	ROMEO		

Flares

- Not all flares or rockets work in the same way, be familiar with those on board.
- Flares should be stored in a clearly marked waterproof container, ideally with a pair of gloves, and be instantly available.
- Check for expiry at the beginning of the season.

Red parachute rockets

- These are designed for long range alerting, day or night.
- Fire two rockets, one about 1 minute after the first, so an observer can take a bearing.
- Fire 15° downwind as it will naturally climb into the wind.
- Avoid the rigging.

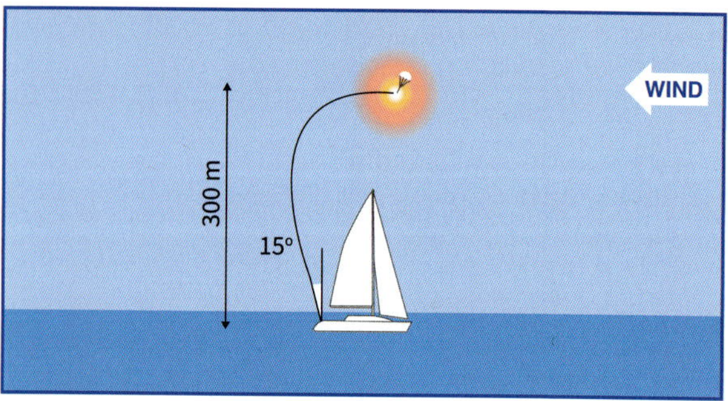

Red hand-held flares

- Can be used to raise the alarm, day or night, at a range of about 3 miles.
- Can also pin-point your position when help is close.

Orange smoke signals, hand-held or buoyant

- Can only be used in daylight.
- Are particularly useful for signalling to a helicopter as they show the wind direction.
- Buoyant orange smoke lasts for 3 or 4 minutes.

LED flares

- Are not yet internationally recognised.
- Battery operated LED hand flares last for up to 6 hours.
- Can be seen for several miles.
- Produce a red flashing light, but an observer may not realise it is a distress signal.

White flares

- These are NOT a distress flares, they are to show the position of a vessel in a potential collision situation.

Emergency Position Indicating Radio Beacons

An EPIRB alerts search and rescue services by transmitting on 406 MHz via satellites. The system operates virtually worldwide and many EPIRBs have built-in GPS to give a very accurate position.

An EPIRB:

- Must be listed on the Ship's Radio Licence
- Must be registered with the Coastguard, via the EPIRB registry
- Will transmit for 48 hours
- Battery will need replacing after 5-10 years
- Should be taken into the liferaft
- Can be fitted to operate float free

If the EPIRB is operated by mistake, switch it off immediately and contact the Coastguard as soon as possible, giving your position and ID.

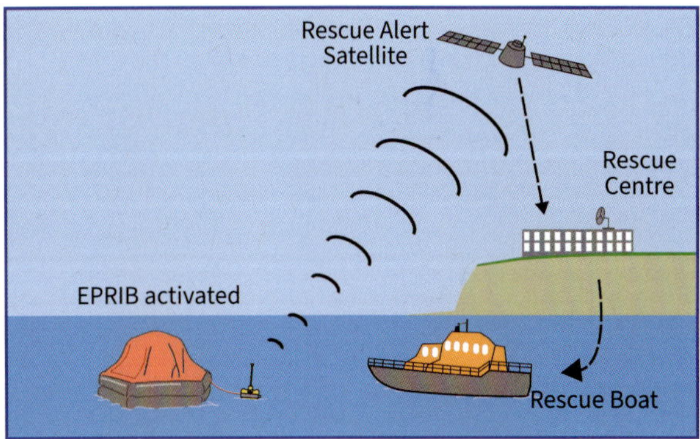

SARTS

Large commercial vessels must also carry a Search and Rescue Transponder or Transmitter for short range emergency location. There are two types:

- A Radar SART is a transponder and responds with a distinctive signal when hit by a radar beam

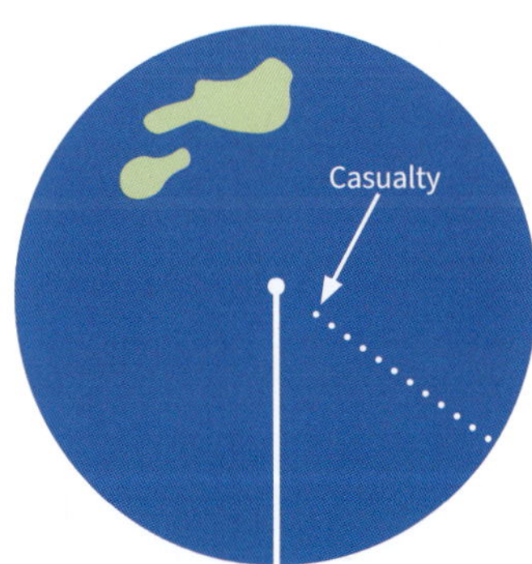

- An AIS SART is a transmitter and places a special target on a chart plotter once activated.

AIS

AIS (Automatic Identification System) is an automated tracking system. It operates in the VHF mobile maritime band. Class A is compulsory for ships over 300 GRT, and Vessel Traffic Services (VTS) ashore use AIS to identify, locate and monitor vessels.

Class B has less functions and is suitable for leisure vessels. Class B can be either:

- Receive-only AIS: will receive information from transmitting vessels nearby and display this on a chart plotter or other screen. It will show the other vessel's position, ID, heading, speed and much else including its MMSI.
- Transmit and receive AIS: a full transponder and will be sending details as well as receiving them.

A skipper should be aware that there is no guarantee that their AIS Class B transmissions will be displayed on the class A set on a ship's bridge. In areas very crowded with small craft operating AIS, the signal may have been filtered out to de-clutter the screen.

AIS information viewed via an App may be subject to delay.

FIRE FIGHTING

Action in case of fire

1. Shout "Fire. Fire. Fire."
2. Everyone on deck, taking the fire extinguishers.
3. Stop the boat: A breeze through the boat will fan the flames.
4. Move crew & the liferaft as far as possible from the fire.
5. Fight the fire immediately.
6. Be prepared to send a Mayday or other distress signal.
7. Remember that water is an efficient extinguisher but not for liquid fires such as fat or diesel.

Fire blanket

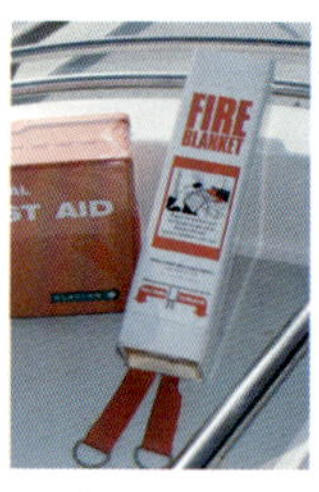

Every boat should have a fire blanket near the galley, but not behind the cooker.

In the case of a fire:

- Turn off gas at the bottle
- Hold a blanket so hands are protected
- Place it gently over the fire and
- Leave it in place for at least 30 minutes

Fire extinguisher

An extinguisher should be aimed at the BASE of the fire, with a sweeping motion.

- Dry powder extinguishers are general purpose, but not recommended for the engine space.
- Have two or three, one by the exit of each cabin.
- Check the gauge regularly and shake occasionally to check that the powder has not compacted.

An **automatic extinguisher** for the engine compartment is recommended. Otherwise at least have a method of firing an extinguisher into the engine space without opening it.

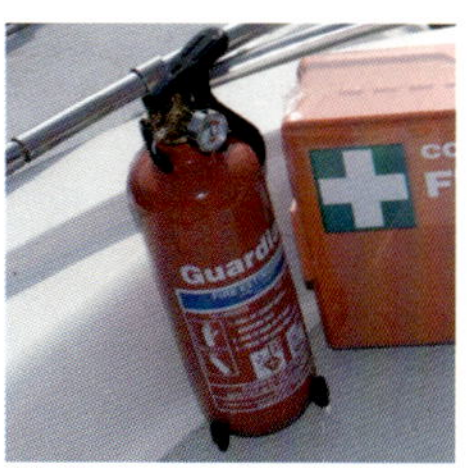

A gas extinguisher is ideal for the engine space as it will not damage the engine.

FIRST AID

Every boat should carry a first aid kit, first aid manual and crew members who have received training.

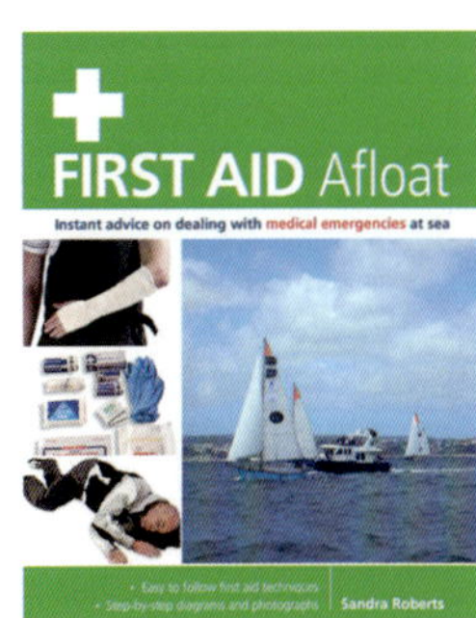

In the case of a life-threatening medical emergency send a DISTRESS ALERT followed by a MAYDAY. If urgent medical advice or assistance is required make a PAN PAN radio call directed to the nearest Coastguard.

PAN PAN, PAN PAN, PAN PAN
Dover Coastguard, Dover Coastguard, Dover Coastguard
This is – *boat name spoken three times*
In position .. *give latitude and longitude*
I require urgent medical advice / assistance
Over

The Coastguard will organise medical advice from a specialist doctor and arrange for evacuation of the casualty by helicopter, assistance from a lifeboat or for the vessel to be met by an ambulance and Coastguard Rescue Team.

First aid kit

In addition to normal first aid equipment useful items to add include:

- Anti-seasickness tablets
- Paracetamol & Ibuprofen
- Aspsirin
- Anti-diarrhoea medication
- Suncream
- Oral rehydration salts
- Anti-histamine tablets
- Laxatives
- Indigestion tablets
- Items required by individual crew members

Afloat be aware of the risks of:

Cold shock

This is the initial response to falling into cold water. The breathing and the heart rate increase dramatically and the casualty is unable to hold their breath. In some cases this will lead to cardiac arrest or inhalation of water. Once this effect subsides, muscle strength will decrease as hypothermia begins and drowning is likely. Once unconscious, even with a lifejacket, drowning will occur as waves splash over the face. A sprayhood is designed to prevent this.

Drowning

A casualty removed from the water should be given CPR if they are unconscious and not breathing normally. For a victim of drowning start CPR with **5 rescue breaths** to increase oxygen to the brain.

Rescue breaths

If CPR is not required treat for hypothermia:

1. Prevent further heat loss. Get the casualty out of the wind if possible or use a TPA (Thermal Protection Aid).
2. If down below, remove wet clothing, provide dry clothes and put the casualty in a sleeping bag.
3. If fully conscious, give warm drinks and sugary food.
4. Monitor for coughing, shortness of breaths or any sign of deterioration which requires medical attention.

Do **not** apply any direct heat, rub the skin to warm them or give alcohol.

Exposure hypothermia

Hypothermia can occur without immersion. The symptoms include shivering, pale cold skin and especially lethargy. Good clothing and watch keeping systems should prevent this, but it can be the cause of accidents, especially if combined with seasickness, dehydration and tiredness.

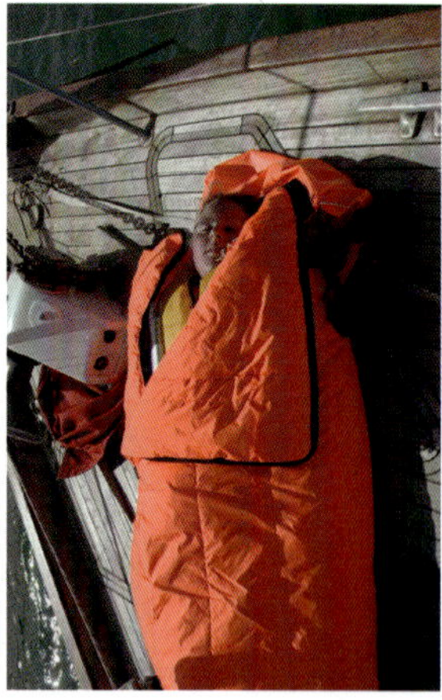

Thermal Protection Aid

HELICOPTER RESCUE

Prepare for helicopter arrival:

- Have orange smoke ready
- Lower or reef the sail, as requested
- Head with the wind 30° to 40° on the port bow
- Clear the deck of loose gear and the port quarter of aerials, dan-buoys, etc.

The helicopter may lower a light, weighted line. Allow this to earth in the water.

Coil the hi-line into a bucket. Do NOT tie it to the boat.

Pull in on the hi-line as the winchman is lowered to the deck.

Ease out on the hi-line, and then cast it clear as the winchman returns to the helicopter.

THE LIFERAFT

DO NOT ABANDON SHIP UNLESS THE BOAT IS SINKING OR ON FIRE.

The priorities in survival situations are:

- **Protection** from drowning and the cold
- **Location** using distress signals
- **Water**
- **Food**

Do not launch the raft too early – it is very unstable initially.

- Prepare the crew with lifejackets, warm clothes and waterproofs.
- Collect the grab bag.
- Check the raft's painter is tied to a strong point.
- Push the canister over the lee side.
- Give a firm tug on the painter, and the raft will inflate.
- Pull the raft alongside, and try to board dry.
- Put a large strong person in first.

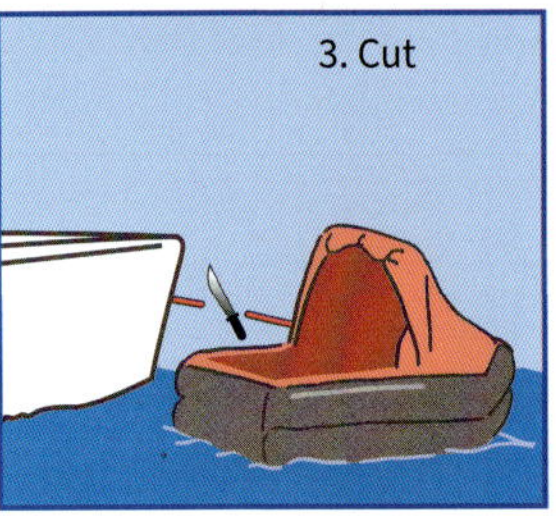

Once aboard, follow this routine:

- **CUT** the painter
- **STREAM** the drogue
- **CLOSE** the door of the raft
- **MAINTAIN** the raft and comfort levels

4. Stream 5. Close

A good quality, well-equipped raft is important, but can be expensive to buy and service. They can be hired for a few days, weeks or the whole season.

A raft can be fitted with a Hydrostatic Release Unit (HRU) so it automatically launches if the boat sinks.

Depending on what the survival pack contains, a grab bag might contain: portable VHF, portable GNSS, flares, torches, leak stoppers / repair outfit, extra clothing, water, bailer and sponge, food, first aid kit, seasick pills, insulating blanket.

TOWING

Towing in harbour

Springs, head and stern lines plus fenders.

or

Towline though enclosed fairlead, or bow roller with pin in place.

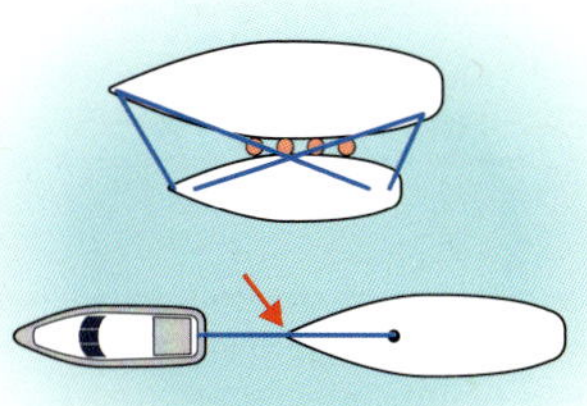

Being towed at sea

Consider one, or all, of these fixing points:

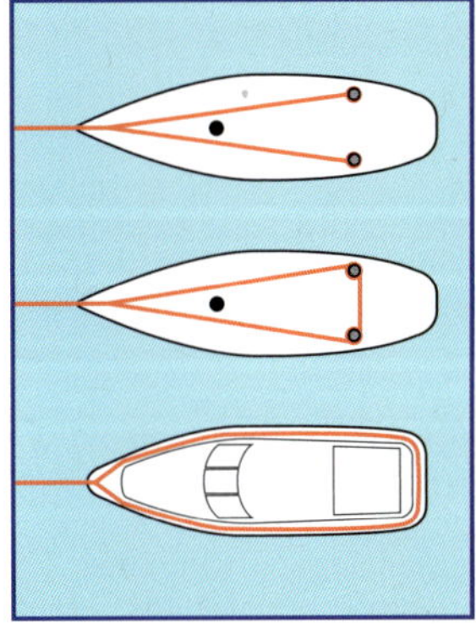

Make a bridle and take to both main winches.

Take the bridle aft, around both winches and back to itself.

For a motor yacht, take around the superstructure.

At the bow either make a bridle or use the bow roller with pin.

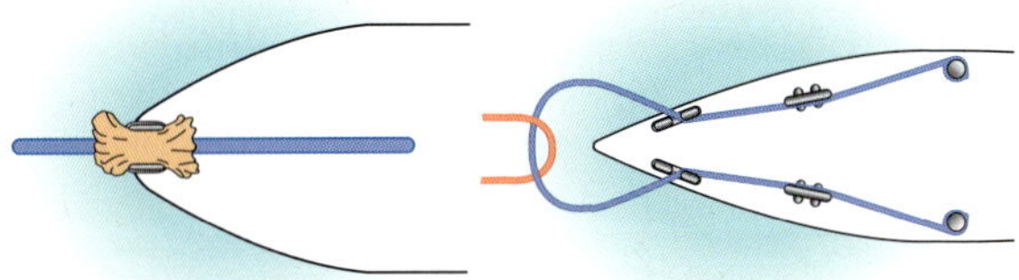

Rope packed with towels to prevent chafe, and secured in bow roller

If no bow roller make a bridle

The boat being towed must be steered and be able to communicate with the towing vessel. If the rudder has been lost, stream a small drogue.

PART 3. NAVIGATION & PILOTAGE

NAVIGATION INSTRUMENTS

The navigation instruments will include steering compass, log, hand-bearing compass, echo-sounder and:

- Chart plotter, integrated with a GNSS, such as GPS, or a basic GNSS
- Perhaps radar and AIS

Global Navigation Satellite Systems

The term GNSS includes GPS, as well as GLONASS, Galileo and other Global Navigation Satellite Systems. These systems update the position every few seconds so can calculate:

- Distance and distance to waypoint
- Cross track distance
- Speed and course over the ground

They have the ability to store multiple routes and can be interfaced to a VHF/DSC and other equipment.

Chart plotters

The chart plotter will use GNSS input to display the vessels position, waypoints and route on an electronic chart and information from other sensors, such as AIS. It may have an auto-routing function to assist in passage planning and many other settings that can be adjusted to customise the display. The system may be a MFD (multi-function display) and be able to monitor additional electronic information. It may be possible to split the screen to show the chart in different scales or to display radar. Care needs to be taken with settings and with zooming as features can be lost. This is especially important when selecting waypoints to form a route. Course over the ground vectors can show progress and cross track distance if the boat deviates from the planned route.

Chart plotter

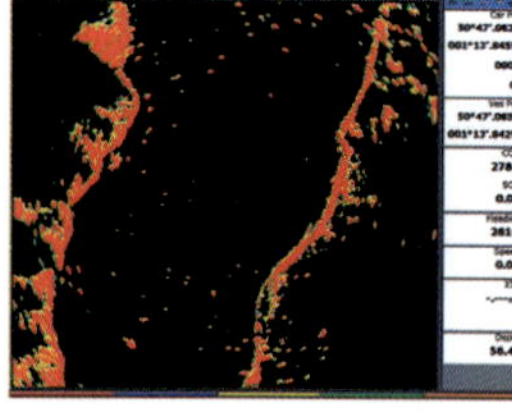

Radar

Radar can be used to confirm the position independently of the GNSS or by an overlay on the chart.

 **All systems vary in capability and ease of use.**

CHARTS

Electronic charts

Electronic Navigation Charts (ENCs) are vector charts produced to International Hydrographic Organisation standards. They are made up of layers of information and can be displayed on a computer screen or on a chart plotter. These charts can be interrogated for extra information and the vessel's position can be displayed directly on the screen using input from a GNSS, such as GPS. On these charts it will be possible to check the Zone of Confidence, in a similar way to checking the source data box on an Admiralty paper chart.

Raster Navigation Charts (RNCs) are also available from official sources. These are a scan of the paper chart, can show only the same information and if over-zoomed they will be unusable. They will be phased out as official vector charts cover all areas.

Unofficial electronic charts produced by commercial companies are also available where the information comes from many sources, including crowdsourcing. This may affect reliability. Unofficial charts may use varying symbols, especially how buoys are shown. Example include Navionics, C Map, Raymarine Lighthouse.

Symbols used on official electronic charts

These are not the same as on paper charts and the Admiralty publish the Guide to ENC Symbols used in ECDIS (NP5012). ECDIS (Electronic Chart Display and Information System) is used on ships, and a small vessel ECDIS system is being developed for small commercial vessels. Scan the QR code or visit the link below to view a quick guide to these symbols; www.assets.admiralty.co.uk/public/documents/2023-03/Admiralty-Quick-Guide-to-ENC-Symbols.pdf

Paper charts

The chart title describes the area covered, and the title panel and notes show:

- The units used for depth and height measurements, and the reference points to which they refer. This is usually in metres.
- The datum used, usually WGS84.
- The projection used to create the chart.
- The edition date and small corrections issued since will be listed on the bottom left of the chart.
- The source data box shows the survey date for different areas on the chart.
- Cautions and Notes with important navigational warnings.
- Tidal stream data referenced to a standard port.

Charts to be carried

If paper charts are carried, they need to include small scale charts for passages at sea and large scale for ports and harbours.

Chart corrections

Charts must be accurate and up to date. Corrections can be found on the Admiralty website under the chart number. Scan the QR code or visit the link here to view corrections; www.admiralty.co.uk/charts

Paper charts are being phased out over the next few years as digital charts replace them, and they are likely to become less readily available.

Admiralty chart symbols

It is useful to have a copy of the book *Symbols and Abbreviations used on Admiralty Charts*, known as 5011, or Fernhurst Books' *Understanding a Nautical Chart* (which contains 5011) on board.

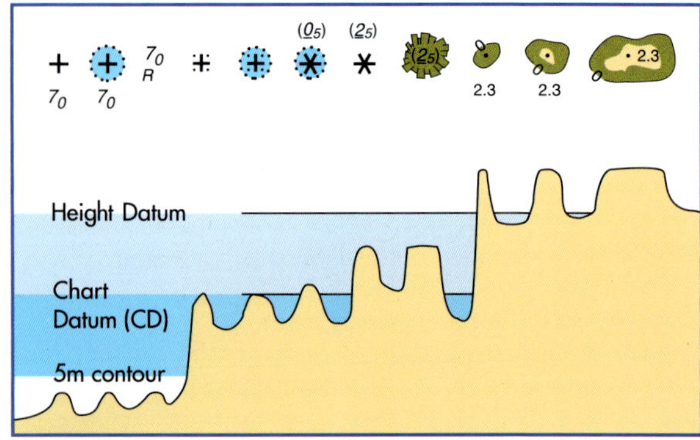

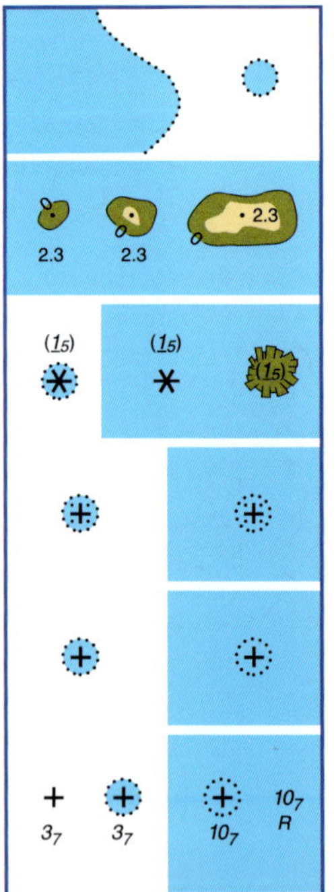

Danger line: draws attention to symbol

Rocks which do not cover, with height above high water, usually MHWS

Rocks which cover and uncover with height above Chart Datum

Rocks awash at Chart Datum

Underwater rocks, dangerous to surface navigation, depth unspecified

Underwater rocks, depth below Chart Datum

Projections

The projection is how the round world is represented on a flat chart.

Mercator's projection

Mercator's projection is the most common as the shape of the land is accurately represented.

- The meridians of longitude are parallel on the chart, rather than converging at the poles.
- The parallels of latitude get further apart towards the poles on the chart, but the distances A, B, C and D are equal on the globe, so when measuring distances from the chart, use the latitude scale in line with the position.

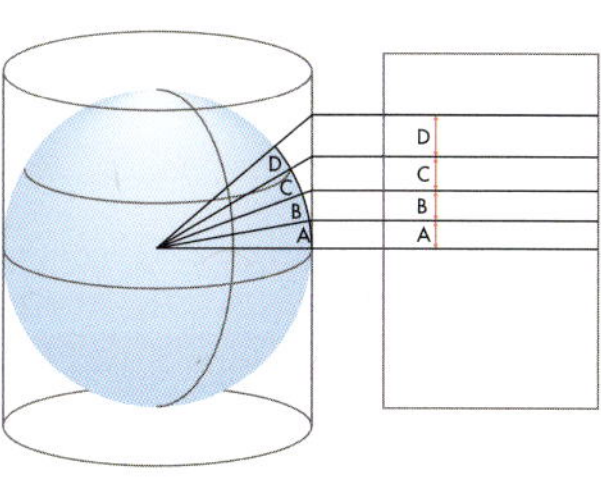

Other projections include:

- **Gnomic projection:** Used for planning ocean passages and, in the past, for polar chart and harbour plans.
- **Transverse Mercator:** Used for harbour plans.

Latitude & longitude

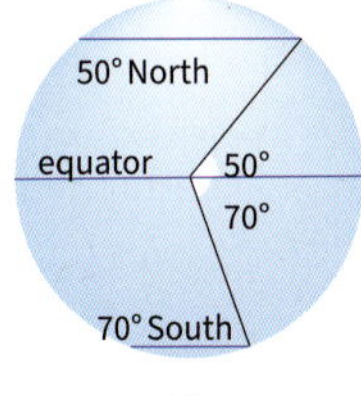

Parallels of latitude

Measured in degrees from equator,
1 degree or 1 ° = 60 minutes or 60'
Minutes are then divided into tenths or hundredths,
e.g. 50° 37'.62 N.

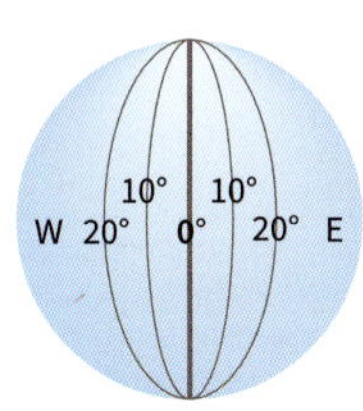

Meridians of longitude

Measured in degrees from the Greenwich Meridian, E and W, up to 180°
e.g. 10° 25'.37 E

Position

Position is given as

- Latitude and longitude
- Range and bearing **from** an object

Distance

1 minute of Latitude = 1 nautical mile = 1 M
1/10 of a nautical mile = 1 cable

Speed is measured in knots
1 knot = 1 nautical mile per hour

COMPASS & BEARINGS

The compass

Variation

Magnetic North is the direction of the magnetic north pole.

True North is the direction of the geographic north pole.

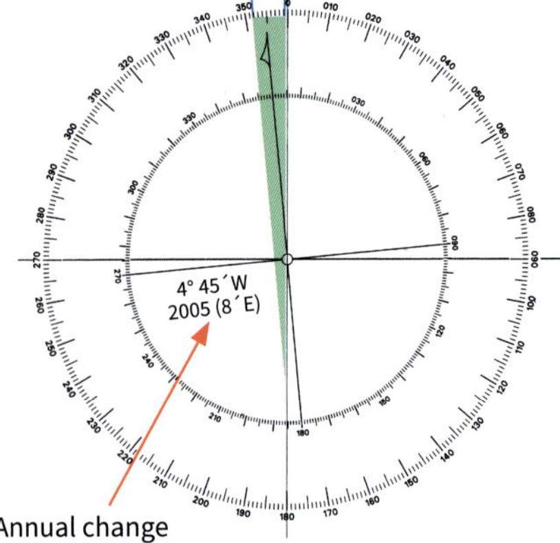

Variation is the angle between true north and magnetic north.

- It is shown on the compass rose on the chart.
- It affects the steering and the hand-bearing compasses.
- It can be E or W.
- It changes with your position in the world.
- It changes very slowly with time.

On this chart it was 4° 45' W in 2005; by 2025 it will have changed by 8' x 20 years, 160' or 2° 40' E, This must be subtracted from the westerly variation, so variation is 2° 05' W in 2025.

Deviation

Theoretically the needle in a magnetic compass points to magnetic north, but the compass in most boats is subject to magnetic interference from the engine, the electrics and electronics. This error is known as deviation.

- Deviation is the angle between the 'correct' reading and the current reading, caused by magnetic interference.
- Deviation can be east or west.
- Unlike variation, deviation varies according to the boat's heading, and for each compass.

Imagine that all the 'interference' in a boat is concentrated into a fixed iron block:

Compass should point here

but iron block 'pulls' it to here: Deviation west

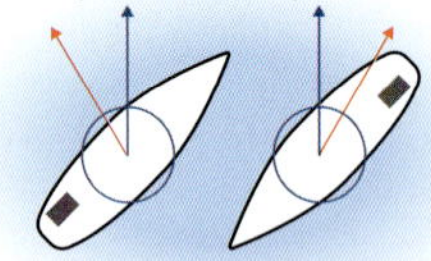

but this time the iron block 'pulls' it to here: Deviation east

It is possible to check for deviation by swinging the compass, or by using transits. A professional compass adjustor may be able to remove it using magnets.

- To swing the compass, point the boat at distant objects on various headings, and compare the reading from the steering and hand bearing compass.
- Transits can be used by pointing the boat along several and comparing the compass reading to the bearing from the chart.

Course & bearings

Courses and headings measured from the chart in True must be converted to Magnetic or Compass for the helmsman to steer. The conversion is done in this order, or the reverse:

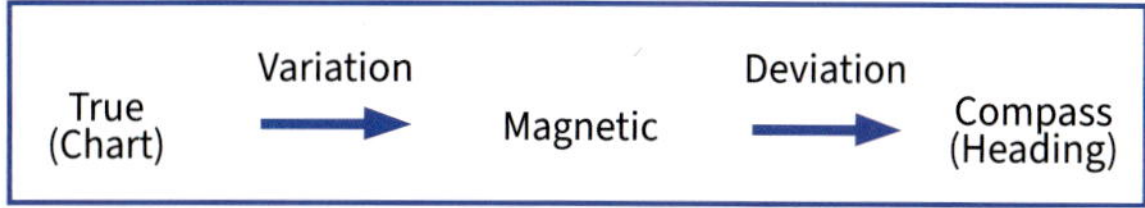

T → v → M → d → C

W+ E–

What is Compass heading for the helmsman?
Course measured from the chart 240° (T). Variation 3° W. Deviation 1° W.

T	v	M	d	C
240°(T)	+3°W	243°(M)	+1°W	244°(C)

Despite the calculation, in practice the helmsman should be asked to steer 245° (C) as its easier to see on the compass.

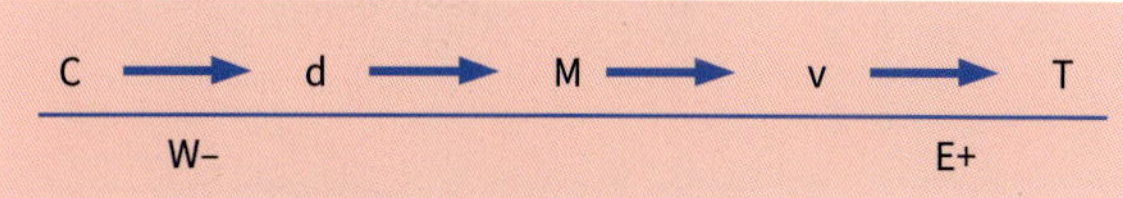

What is True heading to plot on the chart?
Compass heading 075° (C). Deviation 2° E. Variation 3° W

C	d	M	v	T
075°(C)	+2°E	077°(M)	-3°W	074°(T)

Compass error is the sum of Variation and Deviation.

The bearings taken with a hand-bearing will be in (M) as deviation is assumed to be zero.

THE TIDE

Rise & fall of the tide

In most areas there is a High Water and a Low Water every 12 hours 20 minutes, but the size of the rise and fall varies from area to area: from 12 m in the Bristol Channel, to 3.6 m off Harwich.

- **Spring tides** occur when the sun and moon are in line, two days after new and full moon. At springs the high tides are higher and the low tides are lower giving the greatest range. The biggest spring tides occur around 21st March and 23rd September at Vernal and Autumnal Equinoxes.
- **Neap tides** occur when sun and moon are offset, midway between full and new moon. The rise and fall is smallest.
- **Range of the tide**: The difference in height between successive high and low waters.
- **Chart datum (CD):** The level to which depths and drying heights are referred. It is the lowest height to which the tide is expected to fall under normal conditions, known as Lowest Astronomical Tide or LAT.
- **Charted depth:** The depth shown on a chart, the amount of water below chart datum.
- **Height of tide:** The amount of water above chart datum at any time. Shown in tide tables for HW and LW.
- **Charted height:** The height or elevation of a lighthouse above MHWS.
- **Charted vertical clearance** under a bridge or cable is measured above Highest Astronomical Tide or HAT.
- **Drying height:** The height above chart datum of any feature that is occasionally covered.

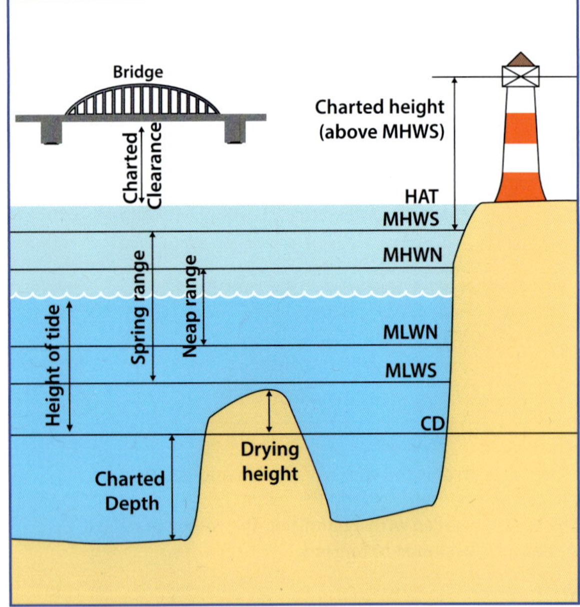

- **Depth of water** at any time:

Height of the tide + Charted depth (CD) OR Height of tide – Drying height.

- **Mean High Water Springs** (MHWS): The average height of all the spring high waters.
- **Mean Low Water Springs** (MLWS): The average height of all the spring low waters.
- **Mean High Water Neaps** (MHWN): The average height of all the neap high waters.
- **Mean Low Water Neaps** (MLWN): The average height of all the neap low waters.

Tide tables

In almanacs and tide tables, predicted times and heights of HW and LW are given for each day for Standard Ports. Other ports are listed as Secondary Ports or sometimes in local tide tables. Predictions are also available online. Scan the QR code or visit this link to find out more: easytide.admiralty.co.uk

Online live tidal data giving the actual height of tide is also available locally through harbour authority websites (e.g. www.hha.co.uk/live-data/tide).

Tide tables are in this form, and are given in UT (GMT) for British waters. In Summer in the UK normally add 1 hour for DST (Daylight Saving Time: BST).

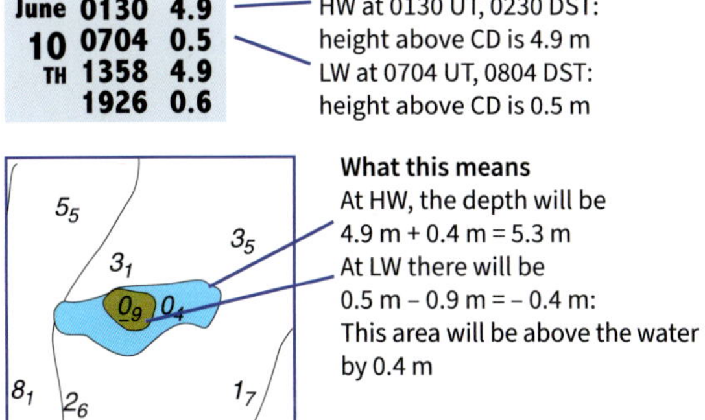

Tide tables for continental ports show local standard time, and in summer 1 hour is added for DST. They also show the correction to convert to UT.

The Netherlands, Belgium and France use CET, Central European Time, or Time Zone – 0100 . This means that 1 hour must be subtracted from the time in the table to convert to UT.

Intermediate times & heights

Without live data intermediate times and heights must be calculated using a tidal curve. It can be used to calculate either:

- The height of tide at a given time.
- The time when there will be a particular height of tide.

The diagram is always set up in the same way:

- Plot the height of HW and LW, either side of the required time, and join them with a diagonal line. RED
- Write the time of HW in the central box beneath the curve, and fill in other times as necessary.

What is the height of tide at Dover at 1600?

1. From 1600 draw a line vertically to the curve (BLUE). The range on the day is near the Spring range, so use the spring curve.
2. Draw a line horizontally to the red diagonal line and then vertically to the height scale to read answer of 5.1 m.

FEBRUARY

	Time	m
16	0136	6.4
	0852	1.1
M	1347	6.1
	2100	1.2

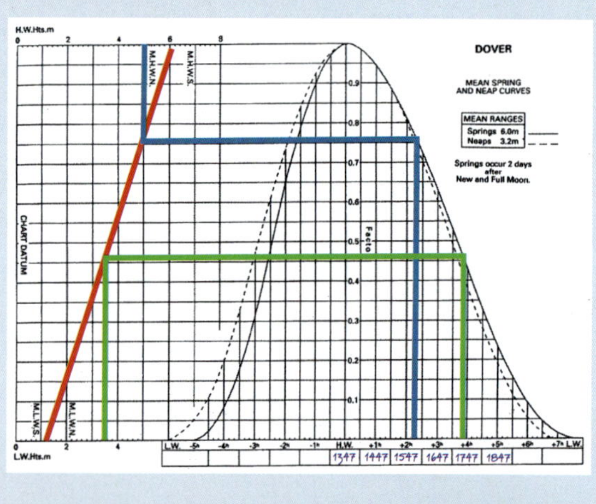

What time after HW in the afternoon will the height of tide be 3.5 m?

1. From the required height of 3.5 m draw a line vertically (GREEN) to the red diagonal line, then across near to the spring curve, in this case.
2. Go down to the time scale. Time is 1737 or so!

Secondary ports

For each Secondary Port there are a set of corrections, or differences, to apply to convert the times and heights of HW and LW from the standard port.

For example: Penzance, a secondary port on Plymouth:

Standard Port PLYMOUTH

Times				Height (metres)			
High water		Low water		MHWS	MHWN	MLWN	MLWS
0000	0600	0000	0600	5.5	4.4	2.2	0.8
1200	1800	1200	1800				
Differences PENZANCE							
–0040	–0110	–0035	–0025	+0.1	0.0	–0.2	0.0

The left hand side deals with the time differences and the right side with heights.

The table is in UT in the UK, so calculate and apply the corrections, and add 1 hour for DST at the end, if necessary. Other countries also use their standard time.

The corrections vary with springs and neaps.

If the time of HW Plymouth is 0000 or 1200, the correction for Penzance is – 40 minutes, but if the Plymouth HW is 0600 or 1800, then the correction is – 1 hour 10 minutes.

The correction for LW is – 35 minutes or – 25 minutes.

When the height of HW at Plymouth is 5.5 m, HW at Penzance will be 0.1 m higher, and when the height at Plymouth is 4.4 m, HW at Penzance will be no higher.

Interpolation is often needed.

For Penzance there is a 30 minute difference between the corrections for a 1200 HW and an 1800 HW. So, interpolating 'by eye' the correction for a HW around 1500 would be – 55 minutes.

Interpolation can be carried out graphically, or mathematically.

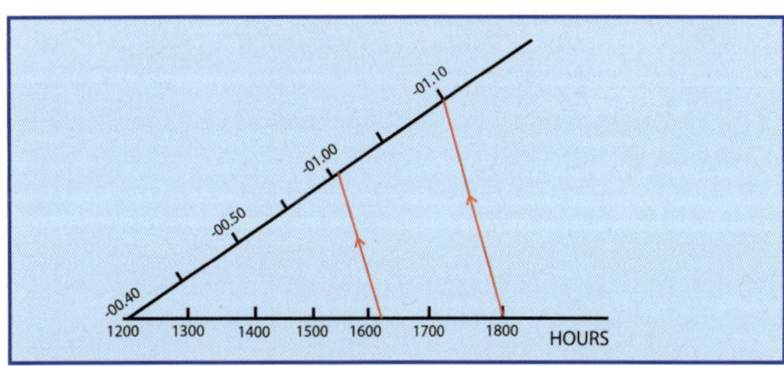

What is the time of HW Penzance when HW Plymouth is 1614 UT?
Calculate in UT, and add the hour for DST at the end, if necessary.
Correction is – 61 minutes, so 1513 UT, 1613 DST.
Similar graphs can be used to calculate corrections for HW and LW heights.

Intermediate times & heights at a secondary port

There are no tidal curves for secondary ports, so the curve for the standard port is used, using the times and height for the secondary port.

Tidal height calculations that might need to be done

Always convert to the secondary port first

What is the minimum depth of water to anchor or moor, to avoid grounding at LW?

1. Find the height of tide at the time of anchoring or mooring using the tidal curve.
2. Calculate the fall of the tide. (height of tide — LW).
3. The minimum depth will be the draught of the boat, + the fall of the tide, + clearance required under the keel at LW.

Will the boat ground at LW on the mooring or at anchor?

1. Find the present height of tide, and calculate the fall of tide.
2. Present depth of water – fall of the tide – the draught = the clearance, if any, at LW.

When will it be possible to get in or out of somewhere not accessible at all states of the tide?

1. Find the height of tide that will be required. This will be:
   A) draught + clearance – charted depth OR
   B) draught + clearance + drying height
2. Use the tidal curve to find when the desired height of tide will be reached.

Aground: When will the boat re-float?

1. Find the height of tide at the time of grounding, on the falling tide.
2. When will the height of tide rise to that level on the next HW?

What will the clearance be under a bridge or cable?

1. Look up the clearance above HAT shown on the chart.
2. Calculate the height of tide.
3. HAT – height of tide = the additional clearance to that shown on the chart.

Local tides

For some areas there is a stand at high water, or two high waters. The curve is based on the more predictable LW. From there proceed as before.

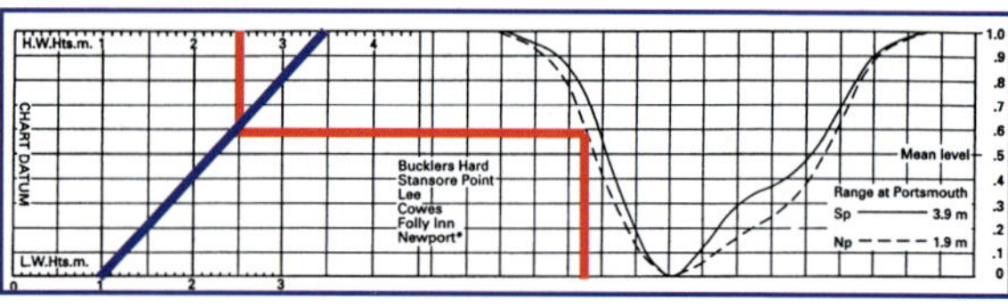

Tidal streams

Tidal streams are the horizontal movement of the water caused by the vertical rise and fall of the tide. They normally change direction about every six hours, although the change is not necessarily at local HW or LW.

- **Direction:** The direction in which a tidal stream is going shown in ° (T).
- **Rate:** The speed of the tidal stream in knots.
- **A tide race** occurs where a strong tidal stream passes through a narrow passage, or passes a headland. These can make it very rough, especially if the wind is blowing in the opposite direction to the tidal stream.
- **Overfalls** are caused by a tidal stream flowing strongly over an uneven seabed.

Tidal stream information

The information is displayed in three ways:

- By interogating an electronic chart
- Tidal atlas
- Tidal diamonds on charts

Tidal atlas

- Very useful for passage planning.
- Come in sets of 12 in Almanacs or Tidal Stream Atlases.
- Arrows indicate direction of stream in ° (T).
- Length and thickness of arrow indicates strength.
- Rate indicated by figures, 04,08 means 0.4 knots at neaps, 0.8 knots at springs.
- Comma indicates position data was recorded.
- Interpolate between springs and neaps, or extrapolate if outside normal range.

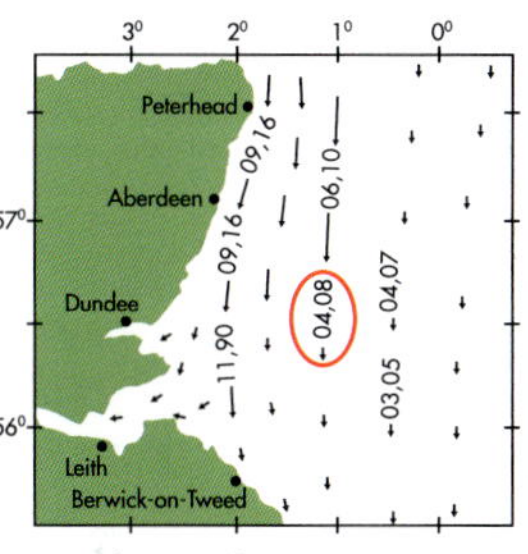

2 hours after HW Dover

What is the tidal stream off Dundee between 1148 and 1248?

7	0359	1.5
	0918	5.9
TU	1627	1.5
	2137	6.0

1. The tidal stream charts are referenced to Dover.
2. Look up HW at Dover, convert to DST, and calculate the range. (HW – LW).
3. At Dover the mean range for springs is 6.0 m and for neaps 3.2 m. (Found on the tidal curve diagram.)
4. Calculate which chart to use, that is how many hours before or after HW at Dover.

5. Measure the direction of the tidal stream from the chart and note the spring and the neap range.
   Tidal stream 183° (T) 0.4 neaps 0.8 springs.
6. On the computation of rates table plot the spring rate on the row of dots labelled spring and the neap rate on the lower row of dots. Join these two up. Measure across from the range of 4.4 m, 5.9 m – 1.5 m, to interpolate between the spring and the neap rate.

The tidal stream is 183° (T) 0.6 knots.

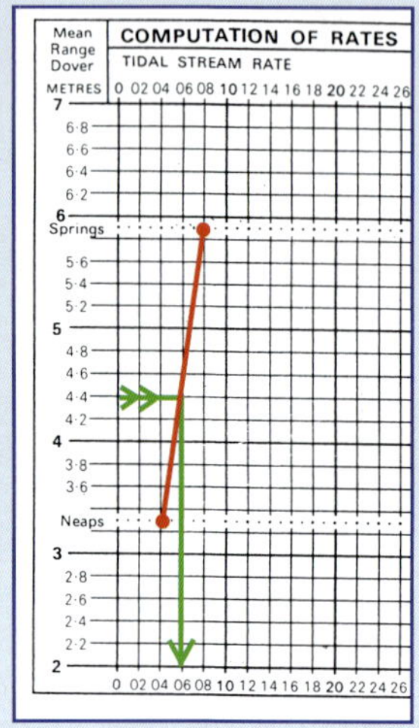

Tidal diamonds on the chart

The information from tidal diamonds appears more precise than the atlases, but is really the same information displayed differently. Tidal diamonds are useful for shaping a course.

Tidal Streams referred to HW at DOVER

Hours		◇ Geographical Position	⟨A⟩ 49°34'ON 6 40 OW		
			Directions of streams (degrees)	Rate at spring tides (knots)	Rate at neap tides (knots)
Before High Water	6	-6	078	0·7	0·4
	5	-5	113	0·6	0·3
	4	-4	160	0·8	0·4
	3	-3	203	0·7	0·4
	2	-2	218	1·0	0·5
	1	-1	237	1·2	0·6
High Water		0	251	0·8	0·4
After High Water	1	+1	283	0·4	0·2
	2	+2	343	0·6	0·3
	3	+3	019	0·8	0·6
	4	+4	033	1·0	0·5
	5	+5	044	0·9	0·5
	6	+6	055	0·7	0·4

2 hours before HW at Dover the tidal stream is 218° (T) at 1.0 knot at springs and 0.5 knots at neaps.

In this case the range is 6.5 m, above the average spring range, but the computation of rate table can be used to extrapolate the rate as 1.1 m.

Dover

10	**0634**	**0.5**	**Range 6.5**
	1115	**7.0**	
F	**1854**	**0.4**	
	2336	**7.2**	

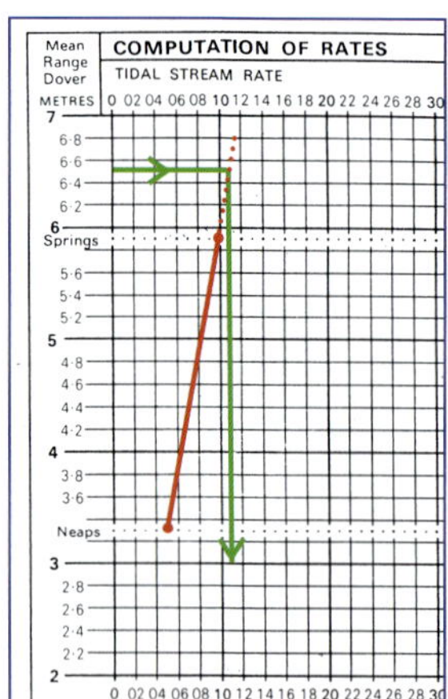

BASIC CHARTWORK

How to find a position

A DR position

A DR position, Dead Reckoning, is based on the direction steered and distance travelled in a given time.

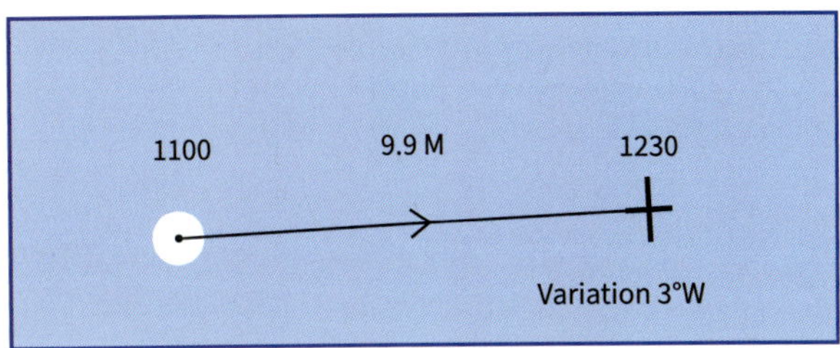

Dead reckoning makes no allowance for the effects of wind or tidal stream.

Leeway is the sideways effect of the wind on a boat under sail, and varies with the wind strength, boat speed, direction sailed relative to the wind, the shape of the boat and how well it being is sailed! Leeway has to be estimated.

The boat is pushed sideways downwind so that its water track is different from the direction actually steered.

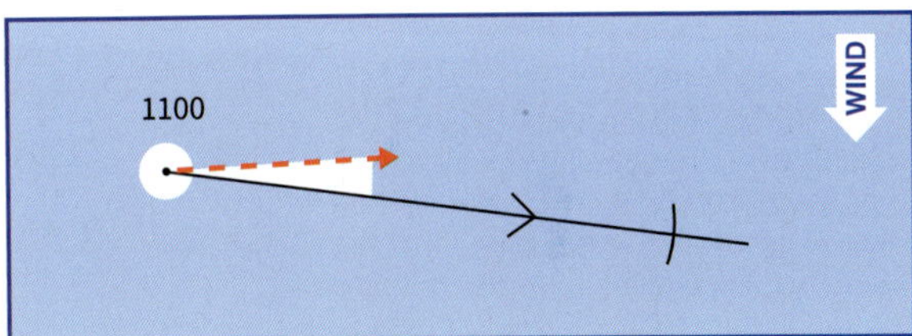

Allow for the leeway downwind, before plotting.

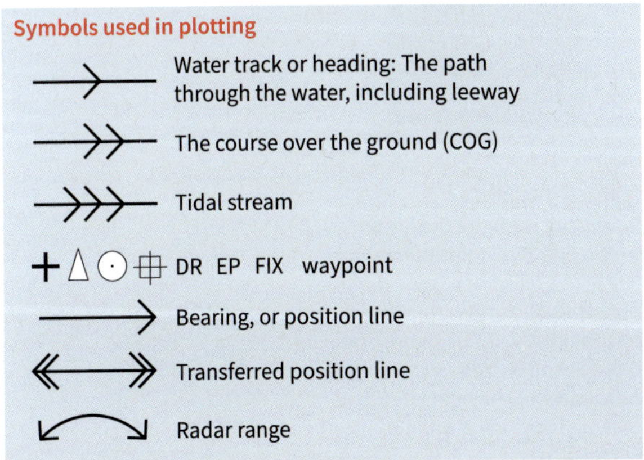

An Estimated Position

An EP is a more accurate position than a DR, as it allows for the tidal stream, and possibly leeway.

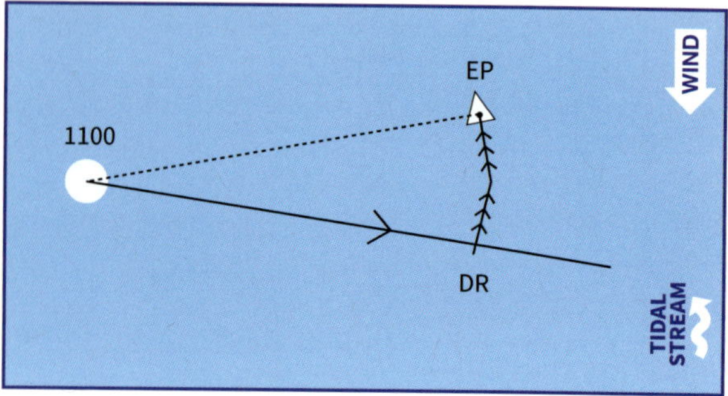

From the DR position plot the tidal stream to find the EP. The diagram will show:

- The speed over the ground (SOG)
- The course over the ground (COG)

by measuring the distance and direction from the fix to the EP.

An EP can also be plotted as a prediction if the heading is restricted by wind direction or if crossing a Traffic Separation Scheme (TSS).

Monitoring your position

1. Using a basic GNSS

- The latitude and longitude from the GNSS can be plotted as required.
- Alternatively, and more quickly, a position can be plotted by using the bearing and distance to a waypoint on the route or an additional waypoint placed for the purpose.

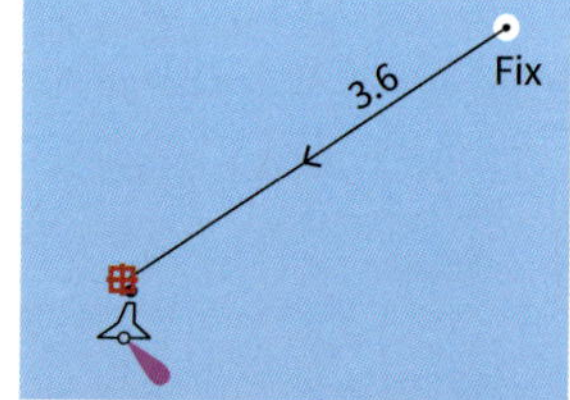

2. Using a radar fix

Radar can measure distance very reliably and 3 radar ranges will give a fix when drawn on the chart as arcs. Radar bearings may not be so accurate due to beam width, and may be relative to the boats heading making more adjustments necessary.

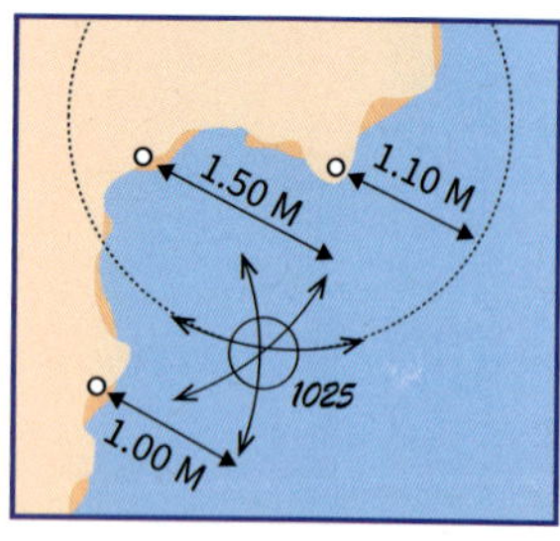

3. Using bearings, transits or depths

Taking bearings

- Chose objects that can be positively identified, and are on the chart.
- Avoid objects too far away as this leads to inaccuracy.
- The minimum angle should be 30° to give a good cut.
- Take care not to make the angle 180° !
- Take the bearing on the beam last as that is changing fastest.
- Land-based objects are best.
- Make a note of the time and the log reading at the time the bearings were taken.

Position lines & fixes

A single bearing of an object is a position line. It is of limited value on its own but can be combined with other information to get a fix.
A traditional fix requires 3 bearings.

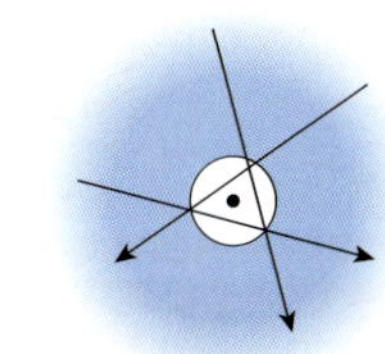

Transits

Two conspicuous objects in line give a very accurate position line, with no need to take a bearing or adjust for variation. Then take a second bearing to give your position.

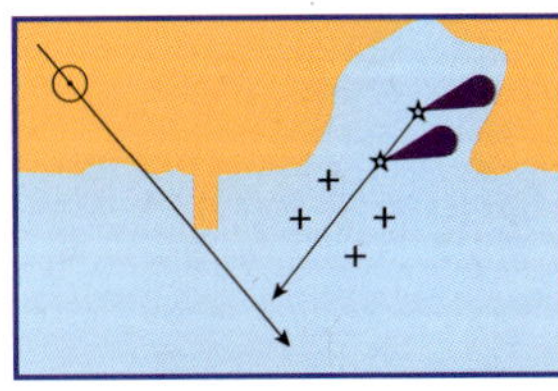

Depth

A steeply shelving sea bed gives an indication of position, but height of tide needs to be deducted.

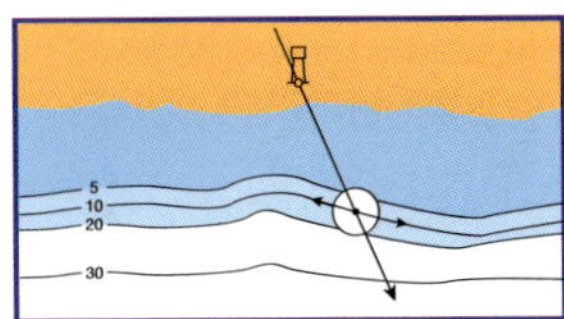

Position by rising & dipping distance

A glow in the sky, known as the loom, can often be seen when the light from a lighthouse is still below the horizon. When the glow becomes a definite light it is said to have risen, and the distance from it can be found in a table in the almanac. If the boat moves away and the light becomes a glow it has dipped below the horizon, and the distance off will be the same.

If a bearing is taken as the light rises or dips, a position can be plotted by finding the approximate distance off in the table using the height of the light and height of eye. This is unlikely to be very accurate.

Running fix

If only one object is available, a fix is still possible by using a transferred position line.

At 1000 chimney bears 045° (T): plot first position line.
At 1100 chimney bears 120° (T): plot second position line.

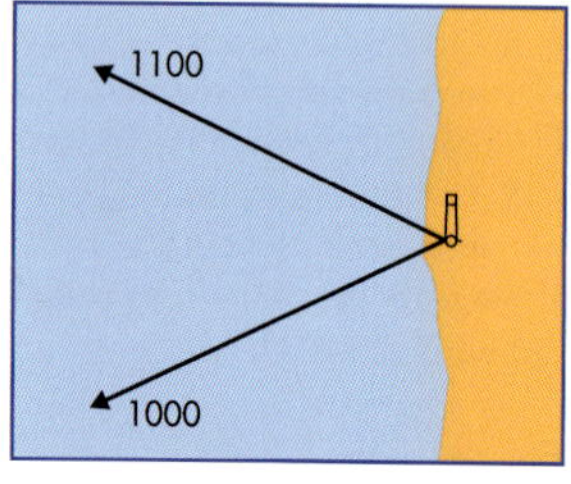

Plot the direction and distance travelled from anywhere along the first position line.
Plot the tidal stream vector at the end, similar to an EP.

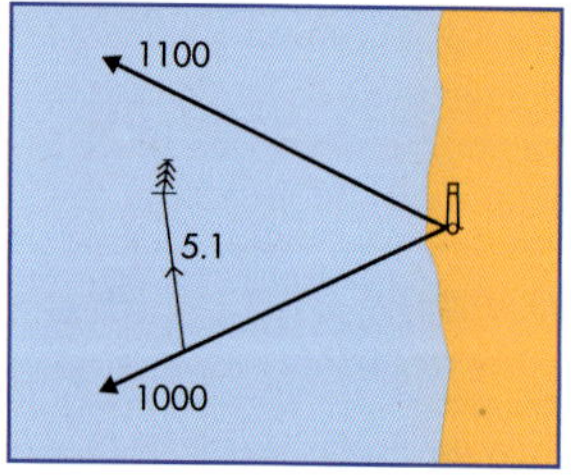

Draw a line parallel to the first position line passing through the end of the tidal stream and the second position line.
Where this transferred position line crosses the second position line is the fix at 1100.

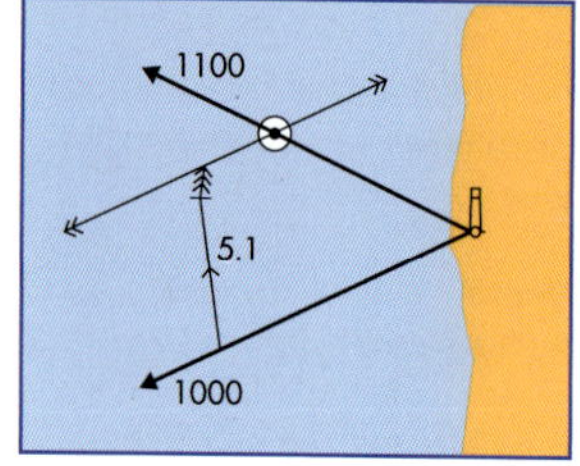

Cross Track Distance (CTD)

The GNSS gives direction and distance to the waypoint. This will not be the same as a calculated course but should be the same as the COG and remain constant, if the predicted tidal stream is correct. CTD will monitor this.

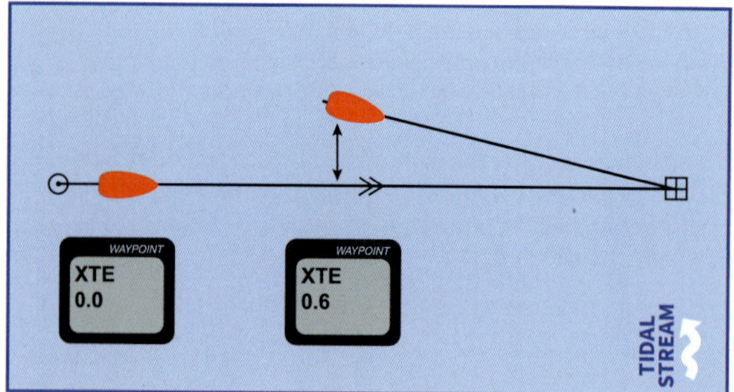

How to shape a course to steer, allowing for the tidal stream

A course to steer is used to find how to get from a known position to a waypoint, allowing for the tidal stream and leeway.

What is the course to steer from the fix to the waypoint?

1. Plot the course over the ground from the fix to beyond the waypoint. Mark with 2 arrows.
2. Estimate how long it will take to get there, using the boat speed. Chose a convenient time period for the diagram, such as 1 hour, ½ hour, 2 hours.
3. Calculate the tidal stream for that time period.
4. Plot the tidal stream from the fix.
5. From the end of the tidal stream line mark the distance that the boat will travel in the chosen time period, and draw a line to that point.
   This is the course to steer.
6. Measure the course to steer and adjust for compass error.
7. If there is sufficient wind to cause leeway the boat should 'head up' into the wind 5° or 10°.
8. A quick look at the diagram shows that the boat will get to the waypoint inside the chosen time period, in this case. A more accurate ETA can be calculated:

$$\frac{\text{Distance to travel}}{\text{Speed over the ground}} \times 60$$

The distance to travel is from the fix to the waypoint, and the speed over the ground can be found by measuring the distance from the fix to the end of the triangle.

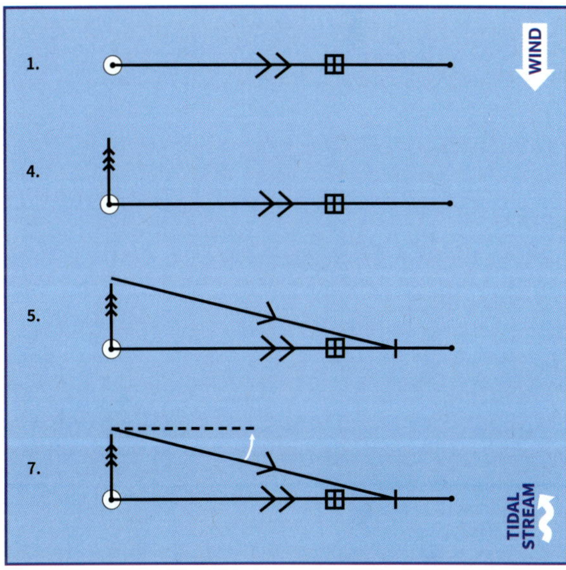

Navigation on a longer passage, approximately 16 hours

1. Calculate the total tidal effect. Here the first 12 hours cancel each other out.
2. Plot a course to steer, to allow for the additional tidal stream, and any leeway.
3. Use the destination as the target waypoint, unless there is a hazard on route.
4. During the first 12 hours monitor the position on the chart plotter or GNSS, and adjust the course if necessary so you arrive at A, to be uptide of the target waypoint.
5. In the last 15 miles monitor the direction to the target waypoint. It should remain constant.
6. Once the waypoint is sighted a bearing or a transit can be used.

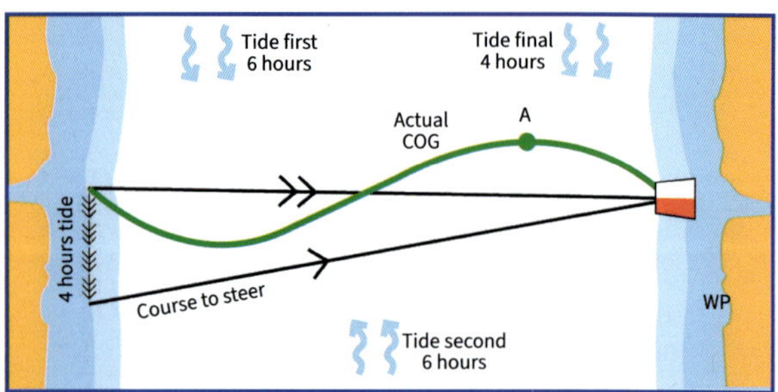

Don't alter course too frequently to remain on the original straight line of the passage, and remember, a one degree change of course gives one mile difference in a 60 mile trip.

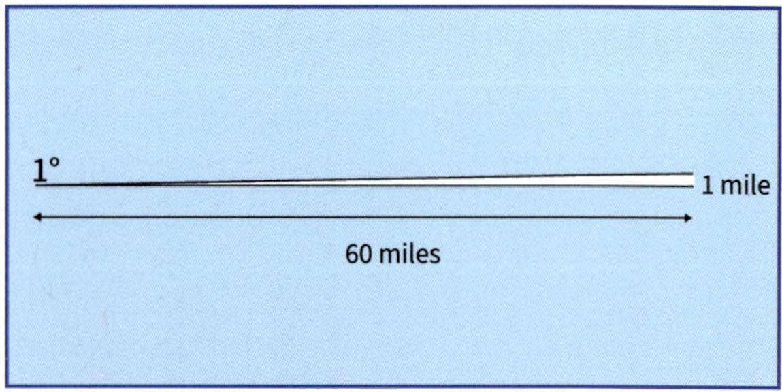

PLANNING A PASSAGE

Passage planning

Making a passage plan is essential and required by the SOLAS V regulations, the Safety of Life At Sea Convention. Certain elements must be considered:

- The weather
- The tides
- The limitations of the vessel
- Crew experience and ability
- Navigational danger
- A contingency plan
- Leaving information ashore

The International Guidelines for Voyage Planning suggest a four stage approach, covering the entire period of the passage from berth to berth.

1. Appraise
2. Plan
3. Execute
4. Monitor

Appraise is the information gathering phase using charts, pilot books and digital sources, as a result of which a **plan** is formed to include waypoints, route, hazards, departure time and ETA and contingency options.

In the **execute** phase the plan may have to be modified due to weather or tidal conditions on the day from live data, or due to a change in circumstances on the boat. **Monitoring** the passage will involve verifying the position with GNSS and other independent means, checking progress against the plan on a chart plotter or chart to ensure a safe passage and timely arrival. This may involve using vectors to show the COG, and alarms for waypoint arrival, XTD (cross track distance) and echo-sounder minimum and maximum depths. If there is a time critical arrival the monitoring may show that the engine should be used, or a change of destination is required. That contingency should be in the initial plan.

Route planning

- Plan the route and select the waypoints. Chose waypoints that can be verified independently with transits, bearings, visual observations, radar ranges or depths. Place them where you expect to alter course or take some other action.
- Give each waypoint a name and save the route on a chart plotter to be used again or reversed.
- Find the courses and distances between each waypoint. If measured from a paper chart and transferred to a basic GNSS, cross check in case of input error.
- Find the total distance and estimate the time for the passage, allowing for the tidal stream and any speed limits.
- If using the auto-routing function on a chart plotter as a first step, zoom in and examine each waypoint and each leg carefully and refine if necessary, especially if warning symbols are shown. Make sure the information about the vessel stored in the plotter is accurate and up to date.

Once the passage planning checklist and routeing are complete it will be possible to decide a time of departure. In particular, consider:

- Any restriction at the ports of departure and arrival, or on the route.
- The best time to get the maximum lift from the tidal stream.

A perfect match may not be possible. It may even be necessary to break the journey and wait for a tide to turn.

CHECKLIST: PASSAGE PLANNING

- ☐ General **weather limitations** for the passage: e.g. lee shore of a harbour entrance.
- ☐ **Weather forecast:** On the day & a few days before to establish pattern.
- ☐ **HW times:** For reference ports for tidal stream atlas & charts.
- ☐ **Tidal stream atlas:** Marked up with time on each map to show when there will be the maximum advantage (particularly important on coastal passages).
- ☐ **Range of tide:** To calculate tidal stream rates.
- ☐ **HW & LW times** & height: For all secondary ports.
- ☐ Possible **entry & exit times** for ports & harbours. (Consider tidal height & tidal stream, daylight, bridge heights, bridge or lock opening times & any local regulations, as well as availability of fuel & other requirements.)
- ☐ **Charts:** Check they are up to date & available for the overall passage & detailed charts for ports & near hazards such as sandbanks.
- ☐ **Length & nature** of the passage: Consider if it is suitable for vessel & crew, including the skipper!
- ☐ **Hazards:** Note: e.g. Traffic Separation Schemes, shallow areas, a tidal race or precautionary area.
- ☐ **Contingency plan:** Look for alternative ports or anchorages if the weather deteriorates or if there is any other reason not to complete the passage. Consider shelter, facilities & when entry is possible.
- ☐ **Information left ashore:** Details of passage & how to contact Coastguard if vessel is overdue.
- ☐ Use **RYA SafeTrx App**.
- ☐ If going **overseas**, check current regulations & requirements.

Download from www.fernhurstbooks.com, search for Skipper's Pocketbook and click on 'Additional Rescources'

LIGHTS & BUOYS

Lights

All lights used as navigational aids have individual characteristics. These are shown alongside the light on the chart, for example:

Berry Head Fl (2) 15s 58m 14M.

The characteristics are always shown in the same order:

- **Rhythm**: The distinctive pattern of light and dark, such as Fl, Oc.
- **Colour:** If no colour is shown the light is white.
- **Period:** How quickly the pattern is repeated.
  Fl (2) 15s means two white flashes within 15 seconds, that is 15s before the pattern starts again.
- **Elevation**: The height in metres of the light above MHWS.
- **Range:** The distance in nautical miles that the light can be seen in normal visibility.

Major long range lights are always white, because white can be seen the furthest.

The principal light characteristics are:

Fixed	Non flashing light	**F**
Fixed	Used as a pair of fixed red or green light, vertically, on the end of a pier	**2FR (vert)**
Flashing	Period of light is shorter than period of dark	**Fl**
Occulting	The period of light is greater than the period of dark	**Oc**
Isophase	Equal periods of light & dark	**Iso**
Long flash	Flash 2 seconds or longer	**L Fl**
Quick	Usually a rate of 50 or 60 flashes per minute	**Q**
Very quick	Usually a rate of 100 or 120 flashes per minute	**VQ**

Lights showing more than one colour

- **Alternating lights** show different colours in succession, as Al WR.
- **Sectored lights** show different colours in different areas, and are used to show safe and dangerous zones, or show safe approach channels.

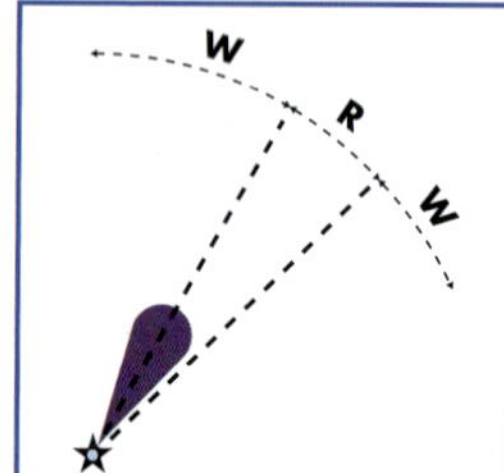

Fl WR 30s 15m 12-10M is a light, flashing every 30 seconds, showing a white or red white light in different sectors. Two ranges are given, as the range of the white light will be greater.

When a sectored light is described in an almanac, the bearings of each sector are given from seaward.

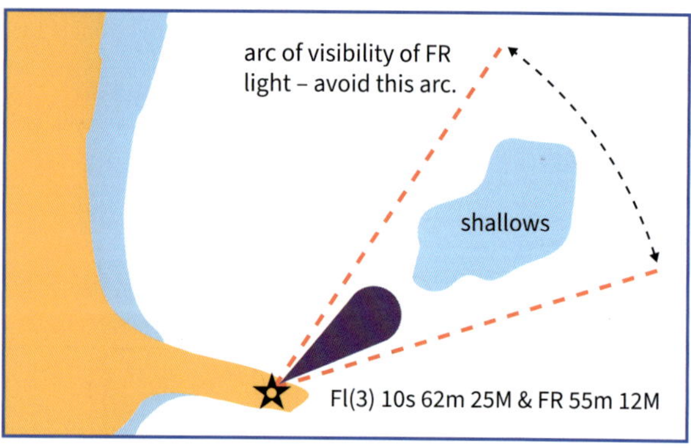

Elevation & range of lights

The elevation of a light is the height of the light above MHWS, in metres.
The actual range at which a light will be seen depends on the height of the light, its power, the height of eye of the observer, and the atmospheric conditions at the time. There are several ways of expressing range, but on charts and in almanacs it is **nominal range** – the luminous range when the meteorological visibility is ten nautical miles. This takes no account of the earth's curvature.

Buoys & beacons

Buoys and beacons are used in inshore waters to warn of hazards and to mark the limits of navigable channels.

A buoy's function is shown by its **shape**, **colour**, **top-mark**, and **light**.

Shapes
Conical, can, spherical, pillar, or spar.

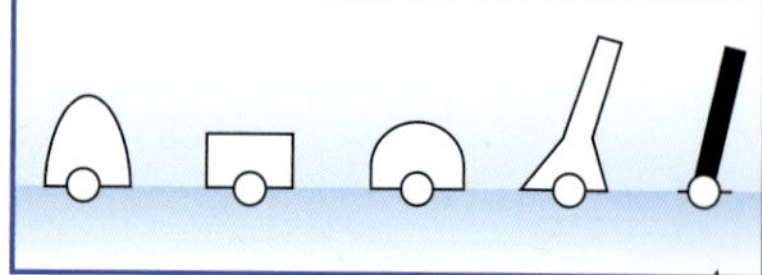

Colours
Normally green (G), red (R), black (B), yellow (Y), white (W), or a combination.

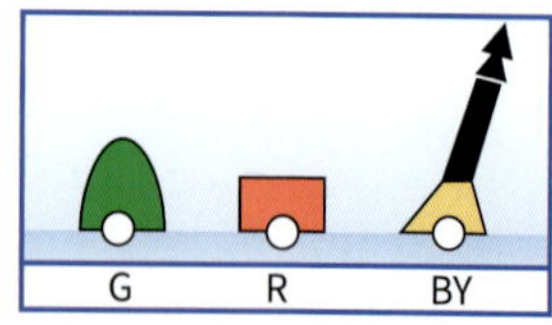

Topmarks & lights
Cones, spheres or cans.
If buoys are lit,  is shown on the chart.

Beacons
In shallow water a beacon may be used in place of a buoy. On the chart these are drawn vertically, rather than at a 15° angle.

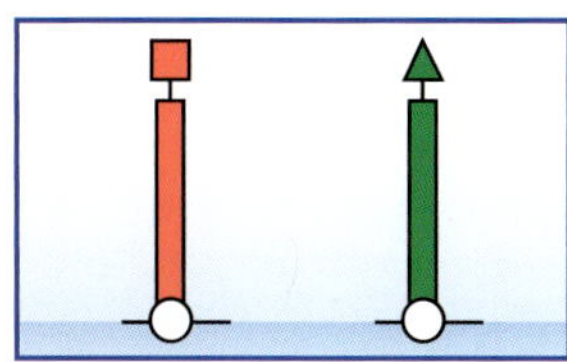

Lateral marks

The systems of buoyage used are known as IALA Region A or Region B. The chart will show which one is being used.

IALA is the International Association of Lighthouse Authorities.

Direction of buoyage: A starboard hand buoy marks the starboard side of the channel when entering harbour. This direction is usually obvious in a river, but where any doubt may exist, a symbol shows the direction of buoyage.

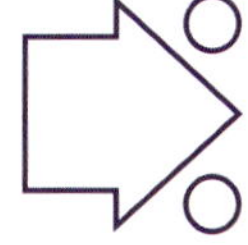

IALA System A (Europe, Australia, New Zealand, Africa, the Gulf & some Asian countries)

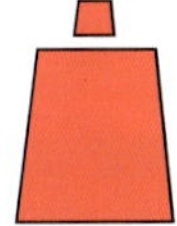

Port hand
Light: red, any rhythm

Starboard hand
Light: green, any rhythm

Modified lateral mark
You could go either side, but one is preferred.

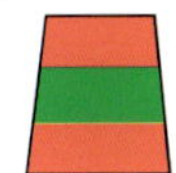

Preferred channel to starboard

Preferred channel to port

IALA System B (North, Central & South America, Japan, North & South Korea & the Philippines)

Port hand

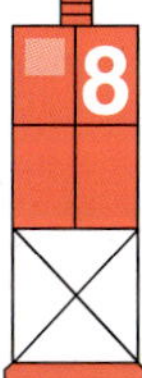

Starboard hand

Cardinal marks

Cardinal buoys indicate the direction in which a particular danger lies, and the side on which it is safe to pass.

- A north cardinal lies to the north of the danger, and the clear water is on the north of the buoy.
- The characteristics of the light follow the pattern of a clock face.

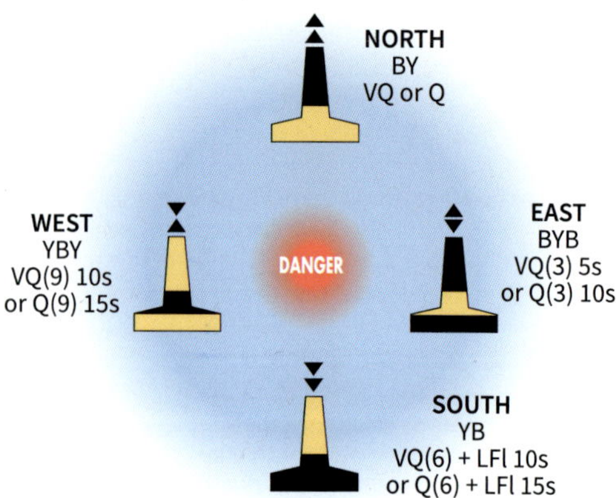

Other marks

Isolated danger mark

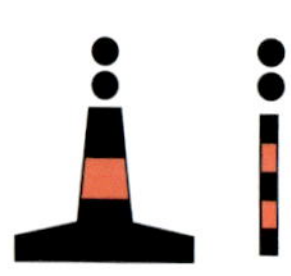

Light: White Fl(2)
Isolated danger with clear water all round.

Safe water mark

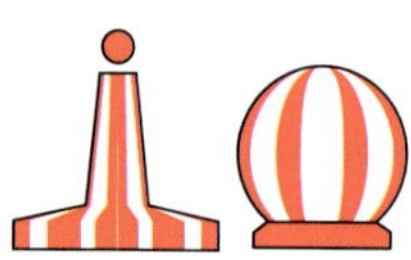

Light: Isophase or occulting or 1 long flash every 10 seconds or Morse 'A' (- —). Usually placed at the approach to a channel: Shows safe water all around.

Special mark

Not a navigational mark but indicating a special feature, such as waterski area or racing mark. Light, if fitted: Yellow. Any characteristic that does not conflict. May be any shape. Topmark, if fitted: Yellow X.

Emergency wreck marking buoy

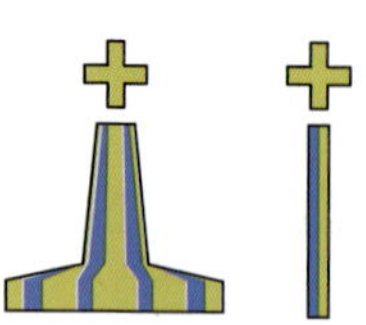

Used to identify new dangers or wrecks. They have blue and yellow vertical stripes and are a pillar or spar shape with a yellow cross as the topmark.

At night, the flashing light alternates between 1 second of blue light and 1 second of yellow light, with 0.5 seconds of darkness in between.

PILOTAGE

Pilotage is visual navigation for a planned port entry using the compass, transits, leading lights or lines, echo-sounder alarms, detailed charts or a chart plotter, radar, while monitoring VHF. When preparing a pilotage plan consider:

- Local regulations, such as VHF channel to use, the need to ask for permission to enter port or observe port entry signals, use of engine or a specific route to follow.
- Whether the tidal height is sufficient.
- Whether the bridge clearance is safe.
- Staying in the buoyed channel at night if there are moorings or moored boats just outside the channel.
- Noting the compass heading and distance from buoy to buoy.
- If a harbour has a complex approach a daylight entry may be advisable. Otherwise include the light characteristic of each buoy in the plan.
- In a busy commercial port it may be better to enter just outside the channel, if there is sufficient depth of water.

Buoy hopping

Following a buoyed channel is the most common form of pilotage.

- Identify each buoy carefully; if one is missed the boat may go aground.
- At each buoy turn onto the next heading.

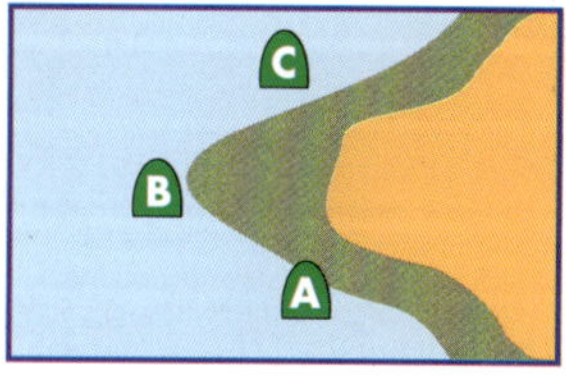

Heading straight for a buoy in a cross-tide can lead to danger. Use a hand-bearing compass or natural transit between the buoy and the background to ensure the boat is on track.

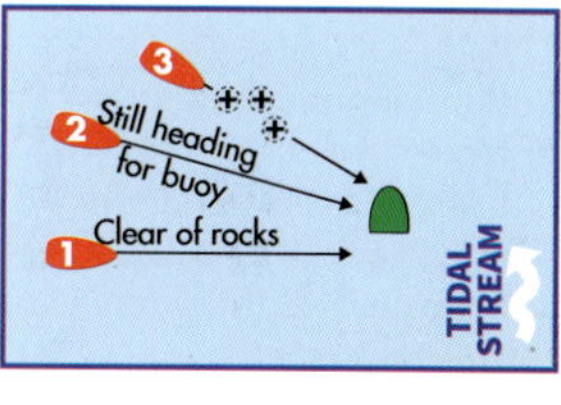

Using bearings

A bearing on the church can be used to enter the bay safely, or as a back bearing for leaving.

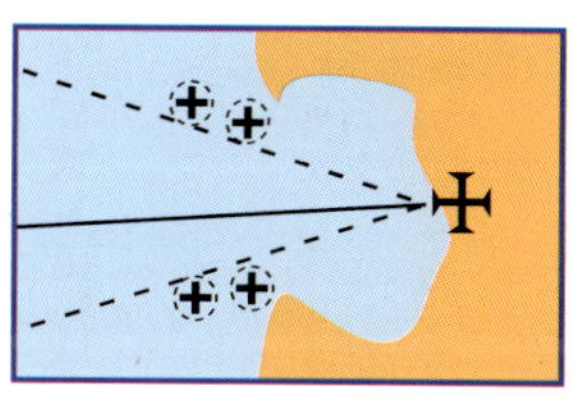

Transit / leading lights

A marked transit or leading lights are established to guide vessels into some ports and harbours. Any natural or man-made objects that line up can be used.

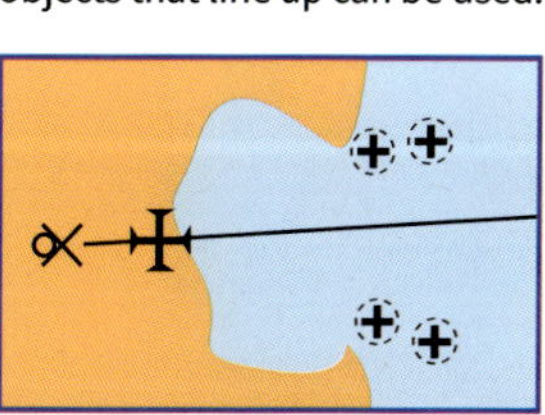

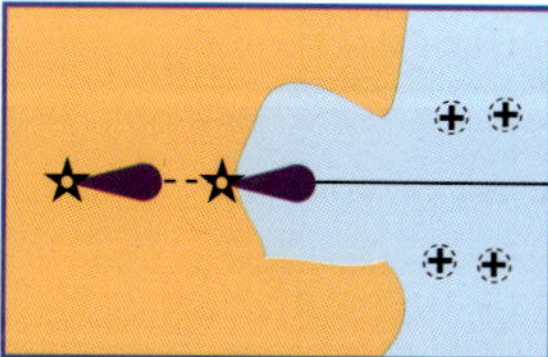

Clearing bearings

Entering harbour the church should bear not less than 005° and not more than 030° to avoid the rocks.

It is possible to tack in, between these bearings.

B
A
No more than 030°
015° is OK
No less than 005°

A clearing transit works well too. The flagstaff must be kept 'to the right' of the church.

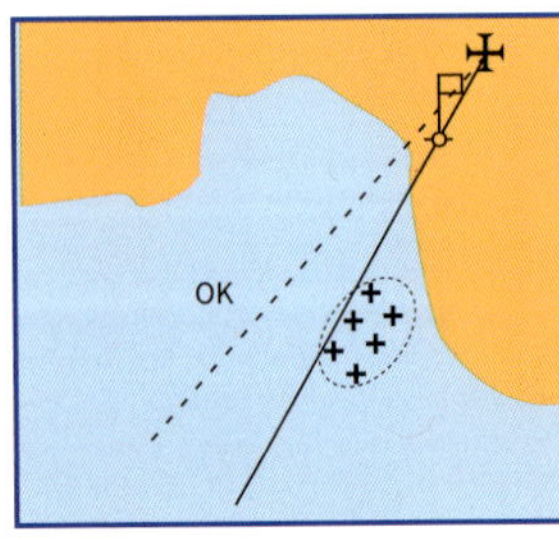

Keep leading light A and B in transit until C and D come into line, then turn to starboard and keep C and D in transit.

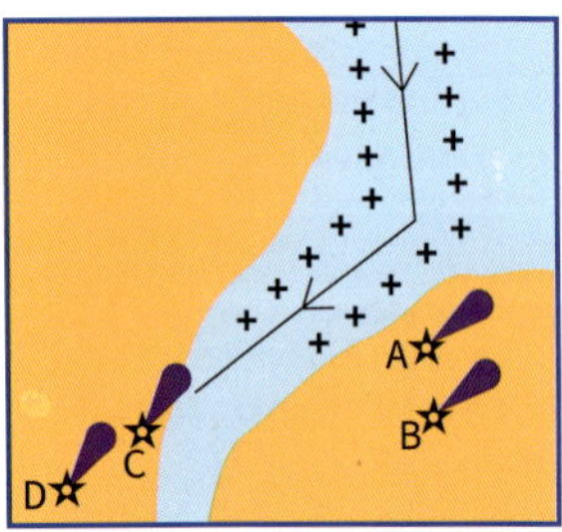

Running a contour

This can be used where there is a shelving coast, with no off-lying rocks.

1. Work out the height of the tide and so the depth on the contour.
2. Considering if the tide is rising or falling.
3. Aim to one side of the harbour entrance, so which way to turn is obvious, and head towards the shore.
4. When the echo sounder gives the required depth, turn towards the destination.
5. Zigzag along the contour to find the buoy.

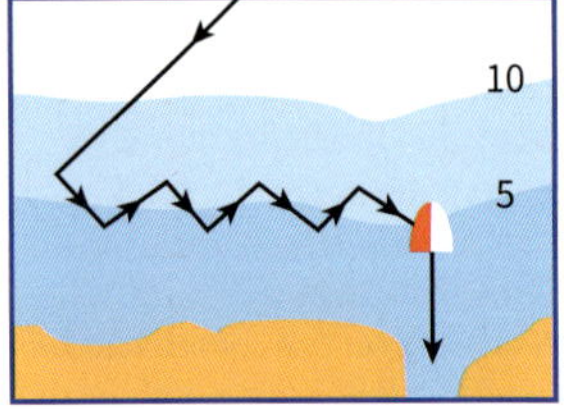

Pilotage plan

It is useful to summarise the plan as a sketch map or plan, noting the heading and distance between buoys.

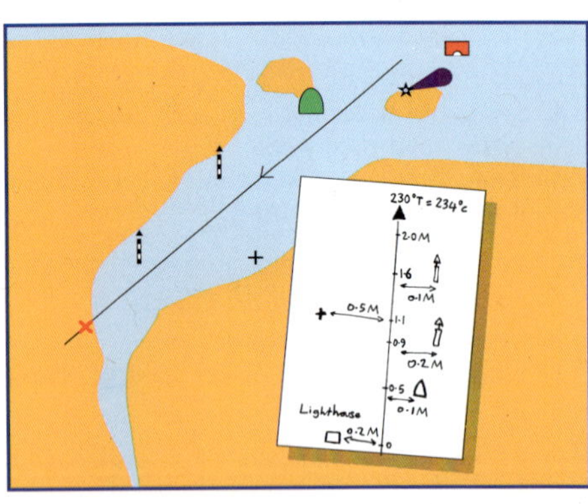

Before making the final approach, check:

- The depth and tidal conditions at the time are safe.
- The weather is suitable to make the entry.
- The boat is starting from a known position.
- The boat is well prepared, and the plan ready.

Arriving at port

At night, buoys may be identified at a greater distance at sea, but near land may be hard to pick out against the background lights of a harbour entrance. Arriving at dawn can solve this.

Sailing in fog

There are three hazards for small craft sailing in fog:

- Being run down by a larger vessel.
- Colliding with another small craft.
- Getting lost and going aground.

If fog is forecast consider taking a different route or whether to make the passage at all.

Actions to consider in fog:

1. Use radar if available.
2. Put on navigation lights.
3. Make sound signals —•• (sail) or — (power) every 2 minutes.
4. Increase lookouts, periodically slow / stop the engine to listen.
5. Keep to a safe speed.
6. Establish the boat's position, consider a change of destination to avoid Traffic Separation Schemes / other busy areas.
7. Make full use of the chart plotter, GNSS, radar, echo-sounder, AIS and monitor the VHF.
8. In very poor visibility, but calm conditions, it may be possible to anchor in shallow water.

The radar reflector should be permanently mounted because a GRP or wooden vessel is invisible without one on the radar of ships. All the crew might need to be on deck, in lifejackets. Use of safety harnesses will depend on conditions.

KEEPING A LOG

It is very important to keep a systematic record during a passage, even if most of the navigation is being done on a chart plotter. This ensures that a position can always be plotted if necessary.

A logbook of some kind is the most efficient way of doing that.

1. Show if time is UT, DST or CET
2. Course being steered
3. Log reading
4. Distance run
5. Relevant data, such as HW times
6. Navigation marks seen, sail and watch changes
7. Alterations of course
8. Barometric pressure
9. Weather forcasts

PART 4.
THE COLLISION REGULATIONS

GENERAL

The full title is *The International Regulations for Preventing Collisions at Sea*, or sometimes just the COLREGS.

The Regulations cover:
- The steering and sailing rules, that is who gives way to whom.
- Lights and shapes, and sound signals.
- The Internationally Recognised Distress Signals are listed as an appendix (see p13 in this book).

Application of the rules (Rule 1 & 2)
These rules make it clear that the regulations apply to all vessels at sea and in harbours, and that additional special rules can be made as well.

Definitions (Rule 3)
- **Underway**: Not anchored, moored, alongside or aground.
- **Making way:** Moving through the water.
- **Power-driven vessel** includes a sailing vessel motor sailing: that is using the engine when the sails are hoisted.
- **Not under command:** A vessel which, through some exceptional circumstances, cannot manoeuvre normally, such as steering or engine failure.
- **Constrained by draught:** A vessel that cannot deviate from its course due to its draught.
- **Restricted in ability to manoeuvre:** A vessel which, because of the nature of the work it is doing, cannot keep out of the way of another vessel. This includes vessels dredging, towing or servicing navigational marks as well as minesweepers, aircraft carriers and other naval vessels involved in certain operations.
- **Vessel engaged in fishing** in the rules means that the fishing activity reduces its ability to manoeuvre.

Lookout (Rule 5)
Every vessel shall maintain a proper lookout by sight and hearing, and all available means, at all times.

This is perhaps the most important rule.

Safe speed (Rule 6)
Every vessel shall proceed at a safe speed so that it is able to manoeuvre in the prevailing conditions. To determine a safe speed the following factors should be considered:
- The state of visibility.
- The traffic density especially of fishing vessels .
- The manoeuvrability of the vessel, particularly the stopping and turning ability.
- At night, the presence of background light such as from shore lights.

- The state of wind, sea and current, and the proximity of navigational hazards.
- The draught in relation to the available depth of water.

Additionally, vessels with radar should consider:
- The limitations of the radar equipment.
- Constraints imposed by the radar range scale in use.
- The effect on radar detection of the sea state, weather and other sources of interference.
- The possibility that small vessels, ice and other floating objects may not be detected by radar at an adequate range.
- The number, location and movement of vessels detected by radar.
- The more exact assessment of the visibility that may be possible when radar is used to determine the range of vessels or other objects in the vicinity.

Risk of collision (Rule 7)

All available means must be used to assess the risk of collision with an approaching vessel. Take a series of bearings with a hand-bearing compass.
- If the bearings do not change a risk of collision exists.
- In the case of a large vessel take the bearings of the stern.

Action to avoid collision (Rule 8)

Any alteration of course to avoid a collision must be bold, so that it is visible to the other vessel. Avoid a series of small alterations of course.
- Take positive action in ample time and with regard to good seamanship.
- At night the heading must change sufficiently for the navigation lights to change as viewed from the other vessel.

Narrow channels (Rule 9)

There is no formal definition of a narrow channel, but any large vessel is likely to consider that the buoyed approach channel to a harbour or port is a narrow channel and expect small craft to keep clear:
- Vessels navigating in narrow channels and fairways must keep to starboard.
- Small craft under 20 m and sailing vessels must keep clear of larger vessels that can only navigate in the channel.
- Do not anchor in a narrow channel or fairway.

Traffic Separation Schemes (Rule 10)

These are established in areas where there is heavy shipping traffic and they are shown on charts.
- Small craft should, if possible, use the Inshore Traffic Zones.
- If small craft have to use a shipping lane they must follow the direction for the lane and they must not impede larger vessels.
- If it is necessary to cross a shipping lane, the **heading** must be at right angles to the lane, and the boat should cross at a reasonable speed, keeping clear of other vessels.
- Don't anchor in or near a Traffic Separation Scheme.

Crossing a Traffic Separation Scheme at right angles

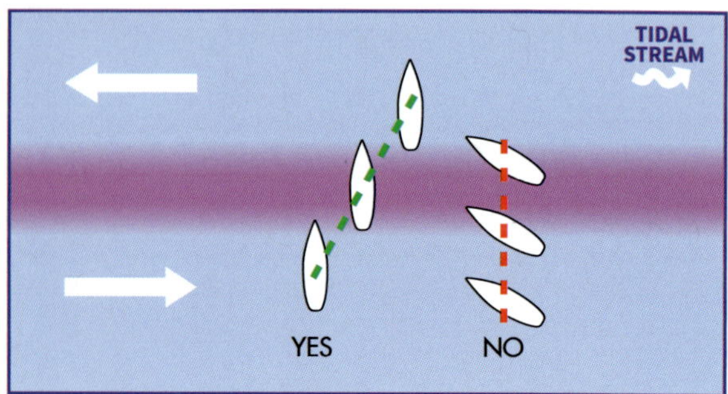

THE BASIC STEERING & SAILING RULES FOR VESSELS IN SIGHT OF ONE ANOTHER

Both vessels under sail (Rule 12)

1. When each has the wind on a different side:
   Port tack gives way, Starboard is the stand-on vessel
2. When both vessels have the wind on the same side:
   Windward vessel gives way

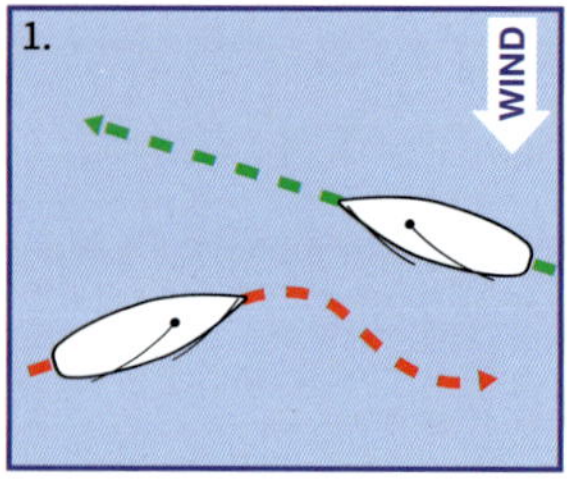

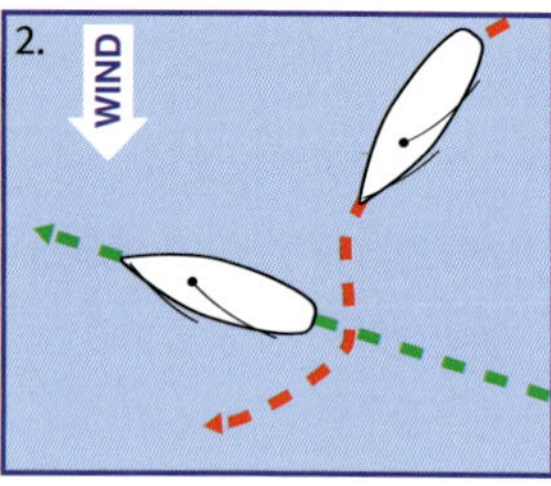

If a vessel is sailing to windward and cannot determine the tack of an approaching vessel:

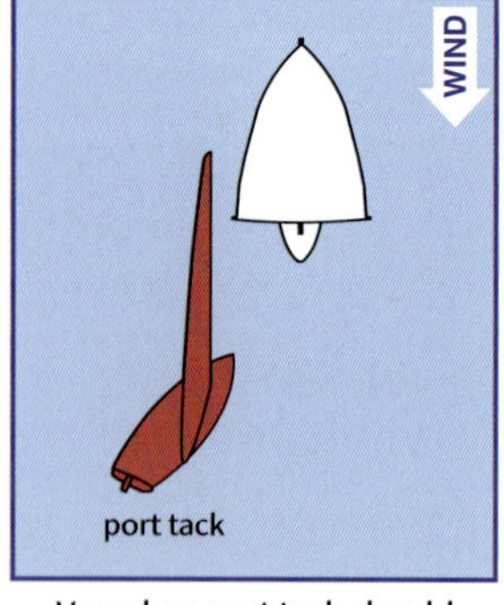

Vessel on port tack should give way

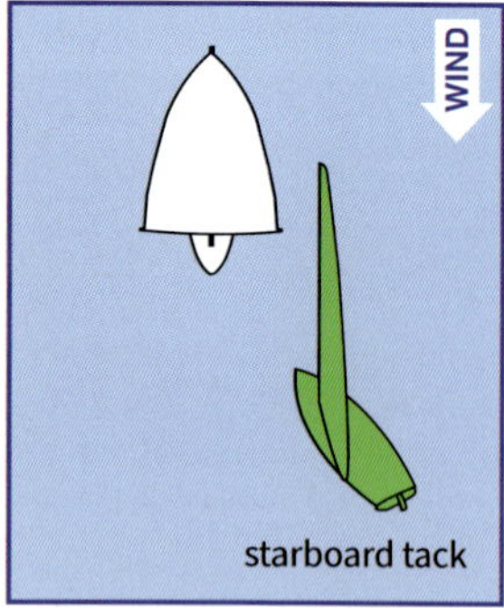

Vessel on a starboard tack should stand on, with care

Overtaking (rule 13)

An overtaking vessel, power or sail, must keep clear of the vessel being overtaken. This rule takes precedence.

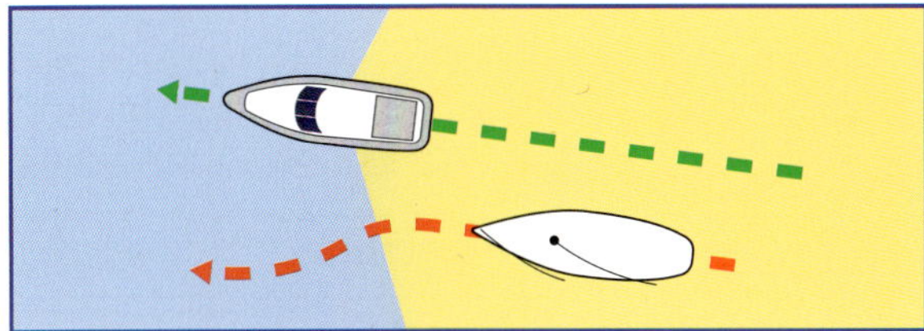

Vessels under power (Rule 14 & 15)

Head-on situation

- Power-driven vessels approaching head-on should both alter course to starboard, and pass port to port.
- Power-driven vessels may make a sound signal when they alter course.

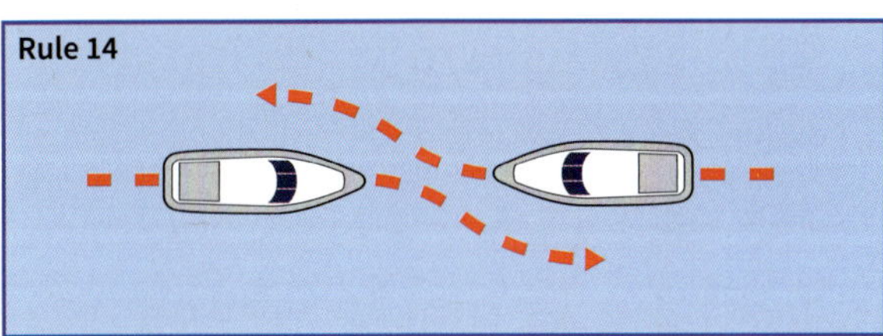

Crossing situation

- If two power-driven vessels are crossing, the vessel with the other on her starboard side should keep clear.
- Power-driven vessels may make a sound signal when they alter course.

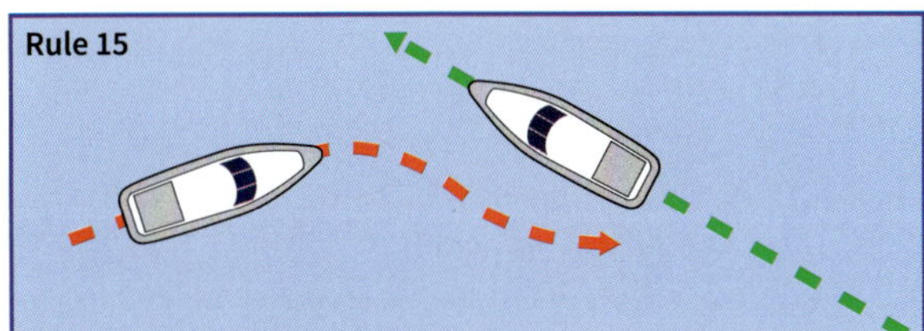

A yacht using its engine, with or without the sails raised, is a power-driven vessel within the rules.

Stand-on obligation (Rule 17)

The stand-on vessel:

- Should maintain its course and speed.
- May take evasive action if the give-way vessel does not, and **must** take action if a collision cannot be avoided unless it does so.
- Should not turn to port for a vessel on its port side.

This rule does not absolve the give-way vessel from its obligations.

Responsibilities between vessels (Rule 18)

The hierarchy

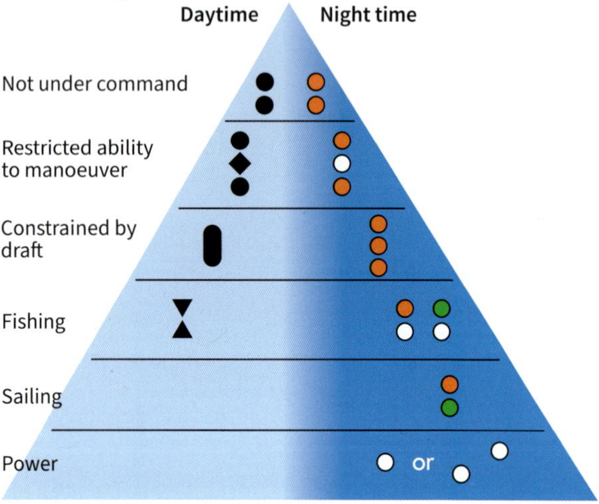

Daytime Night time

Not under command

Restricted ability to manoeuver

Constrained by draft

Fishing

Sailing

Power

or

A vessel must give way to any vessel above it in the list, except in narrow channels, Traffic Separation Schemes and when overtaking.

In other words:

A vessel under power gives way to:

- A vessel not under command.
- A vessel restricted in ability to manoeuvre.
- A vessel constrained by draft.
- A vessel engaged in fishing.
- A sailing vessel.

A sailing vessel must keep clear of:

- A vessel not under command.
- A vessel restricted in ability to manoeuvre.
- A vessel constrained by draft.
- A vessel engaged in fishing.

Small craft – large ships

The Rules may say that, with the exceptions shown above, power gives way to sail, but remember:

- Large commercial vessels cannot stop or alter course quickly.
- Commercial vessels may be travelling quite fast.
- Small craft can be hard to see from the bridge of a large vessel.
- Without a good quality radar reflector, in some circumstances a small vessel may not be seen at all.

Generally small craft should keep clear of large commercial vessels both in confined water and in the open sea – but always making it clear beyond doubt that they are getting out of the way.

VESSELS IN RESTRICTED VISIBILITY

In restricted visibility the normal steering rules do not apply, there is no give-way or stand-on vessel because the vessels cannot see each other.

Restricted visibility (Rule 19)

- Proceed at safe speed adapted to visibility, make sound signals, post extra lookouts, keep a listening watch and monitor VHF.
- Keep clear of shipping lanes and channels, if possible.
- If a fog signal is heard forward of the beam reduce speed to a minimum and navigate with extreme caution until danger of collision is over. Be prepared to stop.

A vessel which detects by radar alone the presence of another vessel must determine if a close-quarters situation is developing and / or risk of collision exists. If so, avoiding action must be taken in ample time. If an alteration of course is made, avoid:

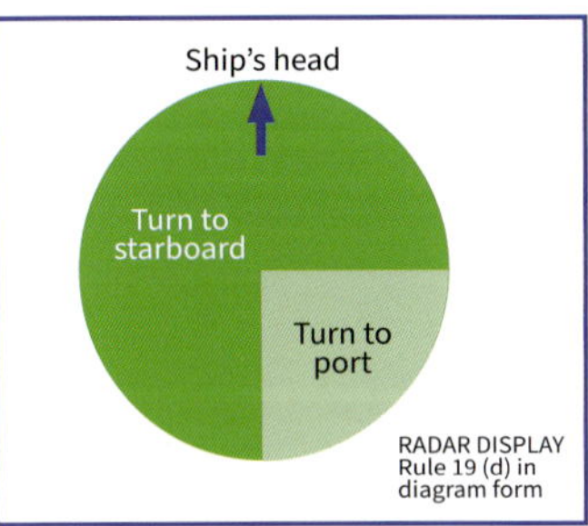

RADAR DISPLAY
Rule 19 (d) in diagram form

- An alteration of course to port for a vessel forward of the beam, other than for a vessel being overtaken.
- An alteration of course towards a vessel abeam or abaft the beam.

LIGHTS & SHAPES

The lights shown by various vessels fit into two categories:

- **Navigation lights**: These are the lights that every vessel must show from sunset to sunrise and in restricted visibility. They vary with the vessel's size and whether power or sail.
- **Distinguishing lights (and shapes)**: In addition to showing navigation lights, vessels in the special categories (not under command, restricted in ability to manoeuvre, constrained by draught and fishing) show special lights.

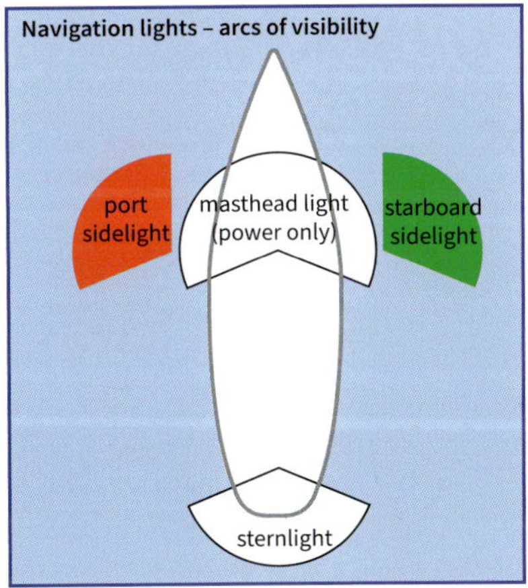

Power-driven vessels underway (Rule 23)

Stern Port side Bow

Over 50 m

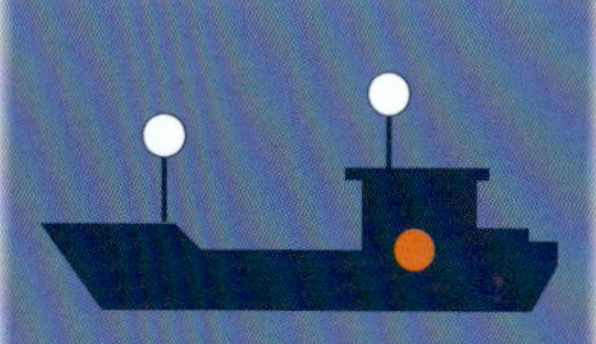

Masthead light – second masthead light aft and higher – sidelights – sternlight

Under 50 m

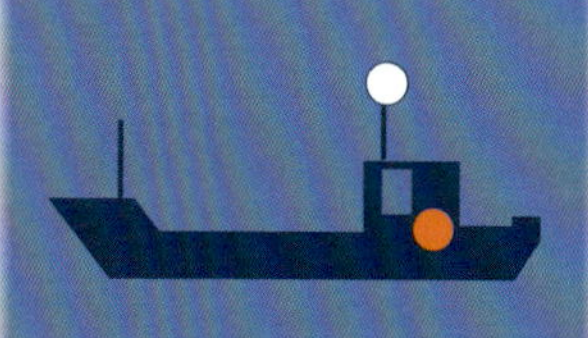

Masthead light – sidelights and sternlight

Under 12 m

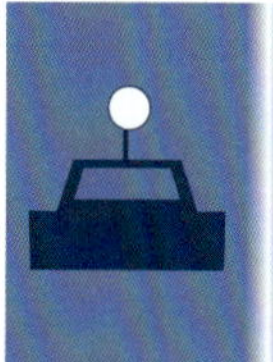
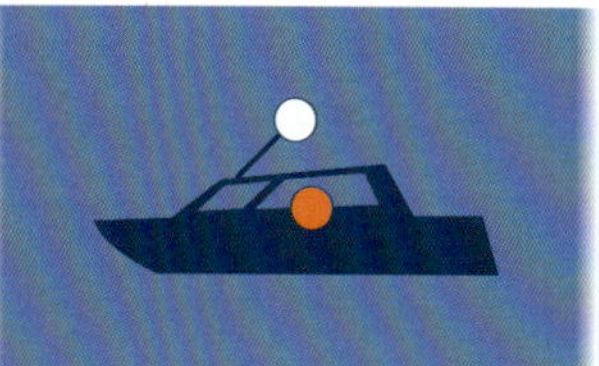

May show all-round white light (instead of masthead light and sternlight) + sidelights

Under 7 m & speed under 7 knots

May show all-round white light only

Vessels under sail (Rule 25)

Stern Port side Bow

Sidelights & sternlight only – no other lights

Under 20m may have combined tri-light (red / green / white) with no other lights

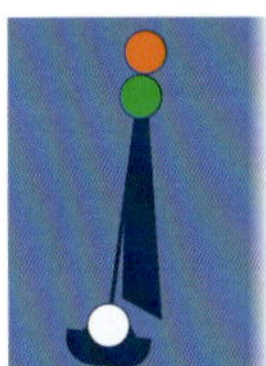
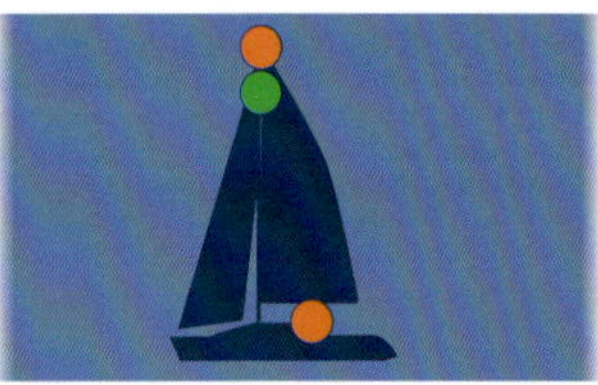
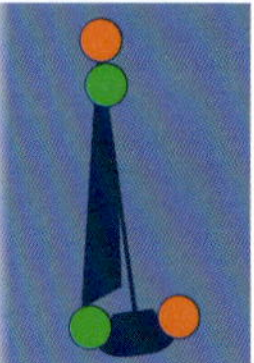

(Rare) A yacht may carry an all-round red over green, plus side and stern lights

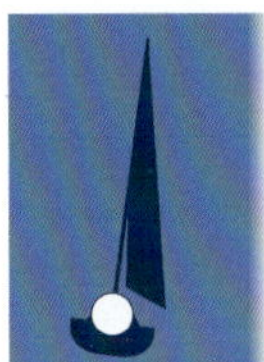

A sailing yacht when **motor sailing** shows the same lights as a power vessel

Do NOT use the tri-colour light at the same time as the side lights & sternlights

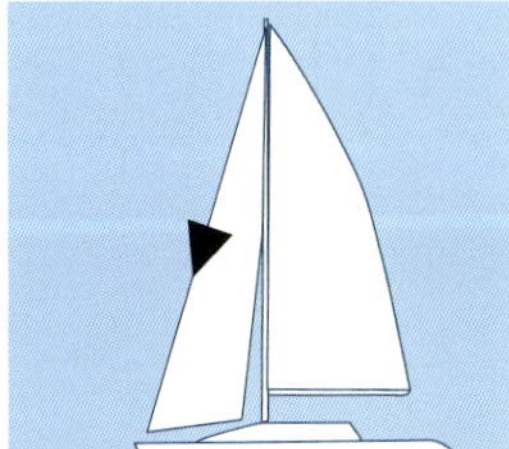

By day: Sailing vessels using their engines but with sails hoisted should show forward a cone, point down

Vessels at anchor (Rule 30)

Under 50 m **Over 50 m**

All-round white light forward

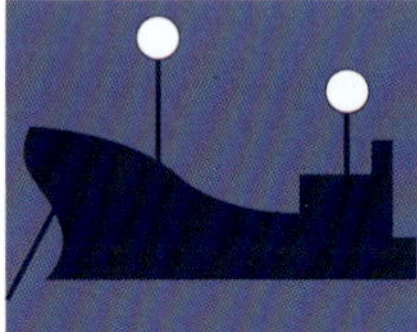

A second white light aft, lower than forward light

By day: one ball

Yachts over 7 m must display an anchor light.
Yachts under 7 m need not, unless near a fairway or anchorage, but it is probably wise to do so!

Vessels aground

Stern Port side Bow

Under 50 m

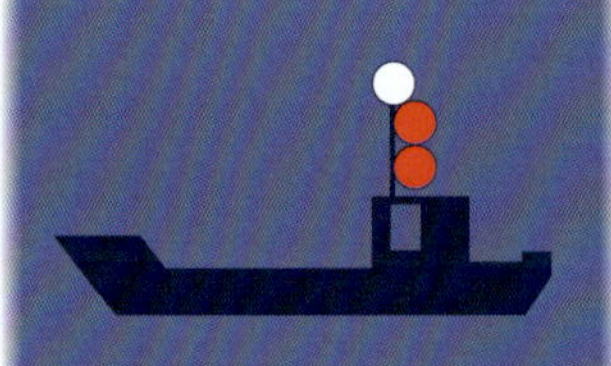

Two all-round red lights plus anchor light

Over 50 m

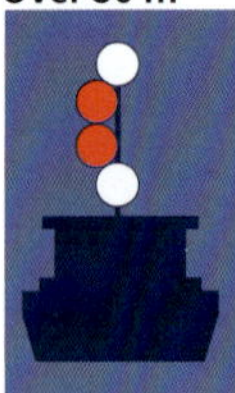

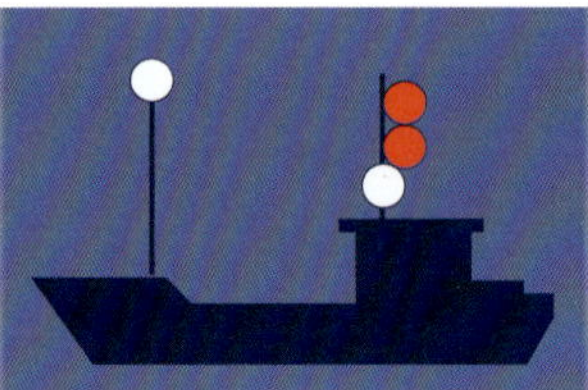

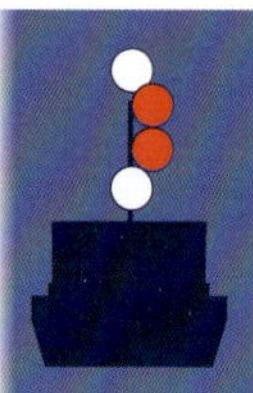

Two all-round red lights, plus anchor lights

By day

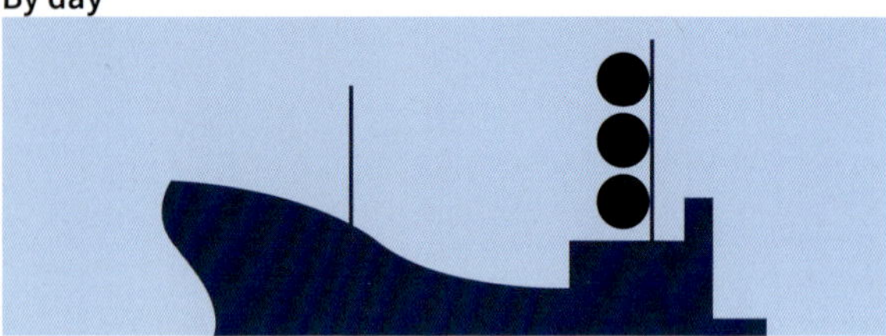

Three vertical balls

Vessels **under 12 m** need not exhibit lights or shapes when aground.

Towing (Rule 24)

The tow is measured from the stern of the tug to the stern of the tow

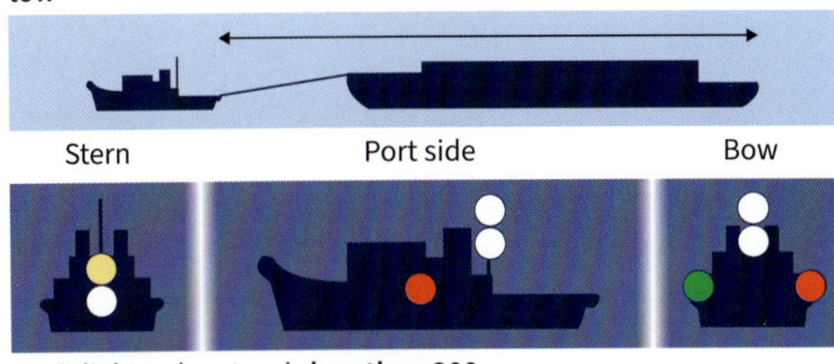

Tug's lights when tow is **less than 200 m**

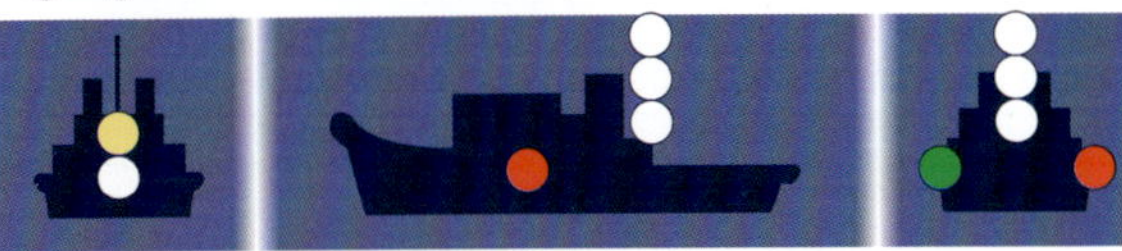

Tug's lights when tow is **more than 200 m**

If the tug is **more than 50 m** it will also carry a second white masthead light aft of, and higher than, the forward one.

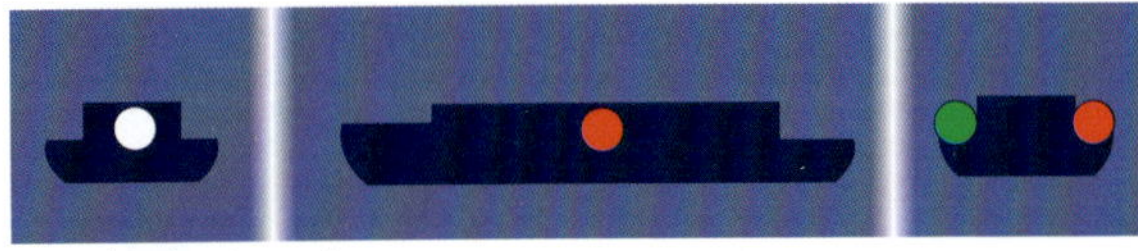

Vessel being towed

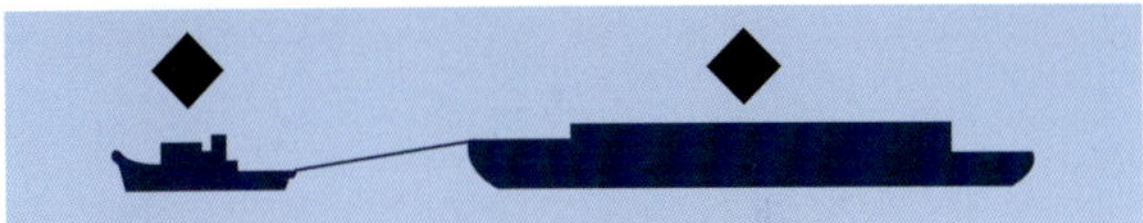

By day: Diamonds only needed if tow exceeds 200 m

Vessels not under command (Rule 27)

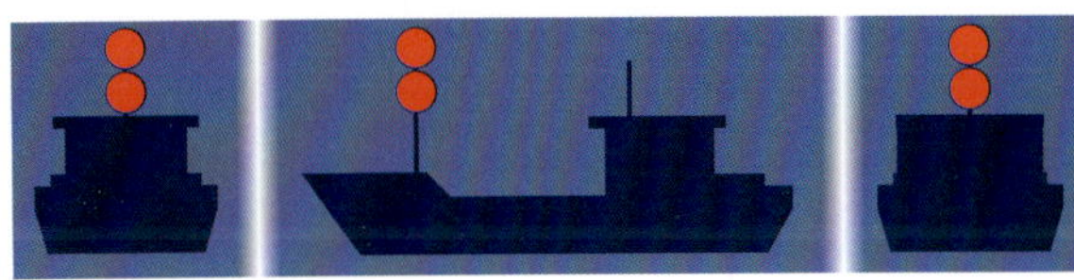

Two all-round red lights

Although it is unlikely that a vessel not under command would be using her engines, she would show navigation lights as well as Not Under Command lights if making way.

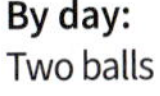

By day:
Two balls

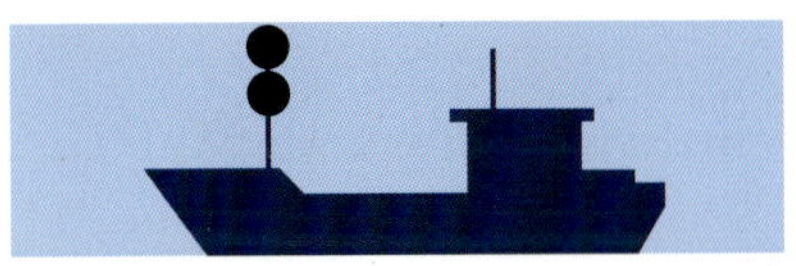

Vessels restricted in their ability to manoeuvre (Rule 27)

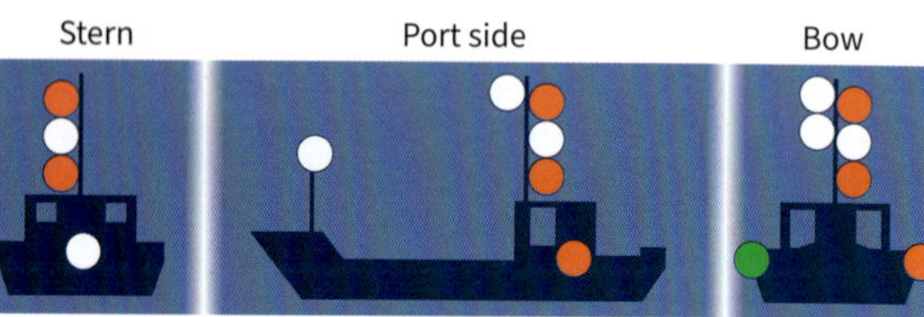

Three all-round vertical lights: red / white / red, plus sidelights etc. if making way

By day, three vertical shapes: Ball / diamond / ball

A working **dredger** shows two vertical red lights on obstructed side and two vertical green lights on clear side (as above) – as well as Restricted in Ability to Manoeuvre lights and navigation lights if making way.

By day: Two vertical balls on obstructed side, and two diamonds on side where it is clear to pass, in addition to Restricted in Ability to Manoeuvre shapes

Diving tender: Flag 'A' or rigid replica

Although diving tenders rarely operate at night, when doing so they must show the vertical red / white / red lights indicating restricted in ability to manoeuvre

Mine clearance vessels exhibit three all-round green lights or balls, plus lights for power vessel or lights / shapes for anchored vessel. Do not approach this vessel within 1,000 m.

Vessel constrained by draught (Rule 28)

Stern | Port side | Bow

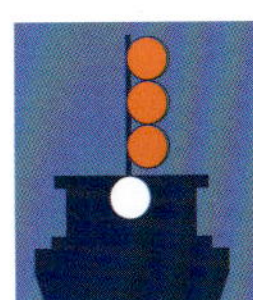

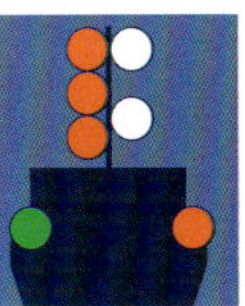

Vessel constrained by draught shows three vertical all-round red lights as well as normal navigation lights

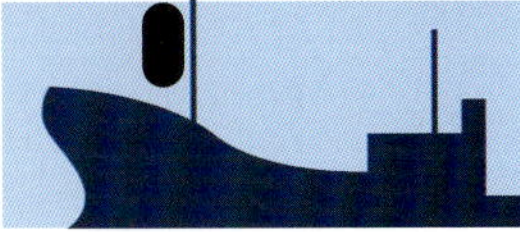

By day: A vertical cylinder

Fishing vessels, trawling (Rule 26)

Vessel trawling

All-round green over white lights. Navigation lights when making way, but not when stopped.

Vessel fishing other than trawling

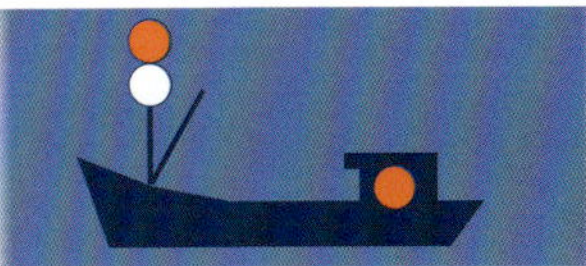
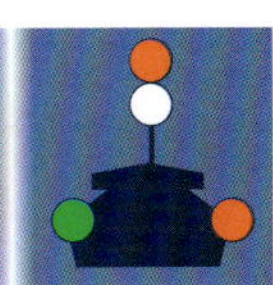

All-round red over white lights, plus sidelights and sternlight if making way.
When outlying gear extends more than 150 m an all-round white light (or a cone – point up by day) in the direction of the gear.

By day: Trawlers and fishing vessels show a shape consisting of two cones with their points together.

Pilot vessel (Rule 29)

By night

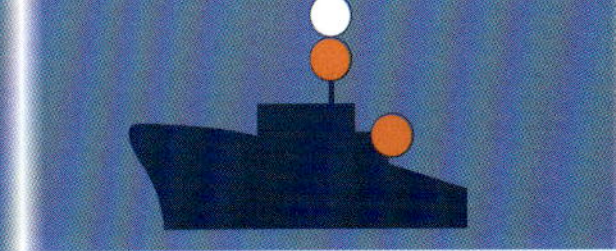

By day

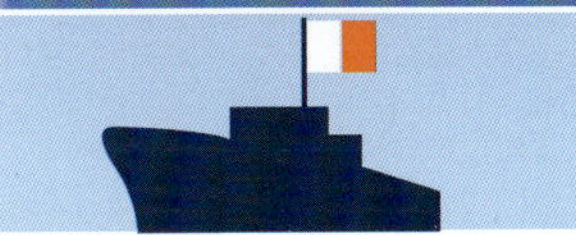

SOUND SIGNALS

Short blast = 1 second = ●   Long blast = 4-6 seconds = ▬

Vessels in sight of each other

●	**1 short blast** Altering course to starboard
●●	**2 short blasts** Altering course to port
●●●	**3 short blasts** Engines running astern
●●●●●	**5 (or more) blasts** Your intentions are not understood. Keep clear.

Vessels in a narrow channel in sight of each other

▬ ▬ ●	**2 long & 1 short blasts** I intend to overtake on your starboard side
▬ ▬ ●●	**2 long & 2 short blasts** I intend to overtake on your port side
▬ ● ▬ ●	**Morse Code 'C'** I agree to be overtaken
▬	**1 long blast** I am approaching a bend in the channel

Note: 1 long blast, in reply, by an approaching vessel.

Vessels in restricted visibility

▬	**1 long blast** every 2 minutes Power-driven vessel underway, and making way
▬ ▬	**2 long blasts** every 2 minutes Power-driven vessel underway, but not making way
▬ ●●	**1 long & 2 short blasts** every 2 minutes Vessels not under command, restricted in ability to manoeuvre, constrained by draught, vessel engaged in fishing and sailing vessel
▬ ●●●	**Morse Code 'B'** every 2 minutes Vessel under tow (if manned)

Vessels at anchor

Rapid ringing of bell for 5 seconds every minute.

Vessel over 100m at anchor
Bell rung forward. Then gong rung rapidly aft for 5 seconds.

Vessels aground

Three rings of bell   Anchor signal   Three rings of bell

PART 5.
METEOROLOGY

THE WEATHER

Four good principles to follow:

- Always get a forecast before going to sea, and for longer passages follow the pattern a week ahead to build up a good picture.
- At sea, listen to forecasts regularly, and watch the sky.
- Monitor and record the barometer on longer passages.
- Relate the forecast to the planned passage, the amount of shelter, the fetch, the tidal conditions, the size of the boat, the heading relative to the wind and consider how it will affect the passage, the comfort of the crew and the safety of the landfall.

Sources of weather information

Before you sail or in marinas:

- **Television** forecasts may be generalised and not marine focused but they give a good, easy-to-understand overview.
- **Radio** provides access to numerous forecasts, including the Shipping Forecast and information from local radio stations. Even the general forecast before the news may give a useful hint about what may be happening a few days ahead.
- **Internet:** The Met Office site provides the Shipping Forecast, maps, the Inshore Forecast and much more. There are numerous other sites.
- **Apps:** There are many including some which give live wind information (e.g. Ventusky, Windy, XC Weather, etc.)
- **Harbour authority website:** Often have live tidal and weather data.

On passage:

- Many **radio stations** will still be available, including the BBC.
- **VHF forecast from Coastguard:** These are ideal when sailing round the UK. Times and channels vary but the information given is for the local area from the Met Office Inshore Forecast. Check in the almanac for the local times.
- **Navtex:** This has the advantage of being very long range, in English, with the information available at any time.
- **Barometer**: A falling barometer, backing winds and high cirrus clouds are signs of an approaching depression.
- **Sky:** Watch for signs of approaching weather system and sudden squalls.

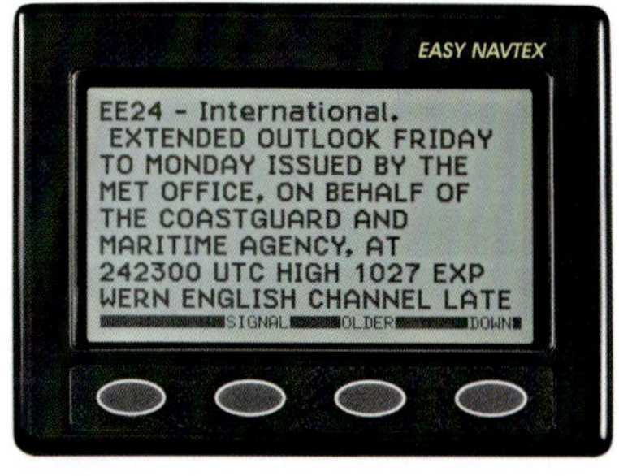

BBC Shipping Forecasts

The Shipping Forecast follows a pattern, using terms which have a precise meaning. The four parts of the forecast are:

- **Gale warnings** in force at the time the forecast was issued, up to an hour before it is read.
- The **general synopsis** which is a description of the weather map about 4 hours before the forecast was issued.
- The **area forecasts** for 24 hours from the time the forecast was issued.
- **Coastal station reports** are given in some forecasts. They contain actual weather conditions recorded shortly before the forecast at specific locations and include information on wind speed and direction, visibility and pressure.

Weather forecast terms

Gale warning:	
Imminent:	Within 6 hours of time of issue
Soon:	Within 6 – 12 hours of time of issue
Later:	Within 12 – 24 hours of time of issue
Gale:	Winds of Force 8 (34 – 40 knots) or gusts of 43 – 51 knots within the area, but may not be over whole area
Severe gale:	Winds of Force 9 (41 – 47 knots) or more

General synopsis:	**Low and high pressure systems movement:**
Slowly:	Moving at less than 15 knots
Steadily:	15 – 25 knots
Rather quickly:	25 – 35 knots
Rapidly:	35 – 45 knots
Very rapidly:	More than 45 knots

Area forecasts:	**Wind**
Wind direction:	Direction from which the wind is blowing
Cyclonic:	A considerable change of wind direction as a low pressure system passes over the area. When mentioned in the shipping forecast in a sea area it indicates the centre of the low pressure.
Veering:	Change of wind direction clockwise, such as SW TO W. (Opposite Southern Hemisphere)
Backing:	Change of wind direction anti-clockwise, such SE TO NE. (Opposite Southern Hemisphere)

Area forecasts:	**Visablility**
Good:	Over 5 miles
Moderate:	2 – 5 miles
Poor:	1,000 m – 2 miles
Fog:	Less than 1,000 m

Other terms

- **Isobars:** Lines joining places with equal barometric pressure.
- **Fronts:** A front is the boundary between two kinds of air.
- **Occluded front:** When a cold front catches up with a warm front the cold air pushes in under the warm air, or the other way round. This occurs as the system begins to decay.

Beaufort wind scale

Force	Knots	Description	Sea state
1	1-3	Light breeze	Smooth
2	4-6	Light breeze	Calm
3	7-10	Gentle breeze	Few white horses
4	11-16	Moderate breeze	Small waves
5	17-21	Fresh breeze	Larger waves
6	22-27	Strong breeze	Rough
7	28-33	Near gale	Very rough
8	34-40	Gale	High seas
9	41-47	Strong gale	Severe seas
10	48-55	Storm	Very severe conditions

Pressure changes in coastal reports
These give the trend over the previous 3 hours. A fall or rise of over 6mb in that time usually means a gale.

Rising / falling more slowly	Pressure rising / falling at a progressively slower rate
Rising / falling slowly	Pressure change of 0.1 to 1.5 mb
Rising / falling	Pressure change of 1.6 to 3.5 mb
Rising / falling quickly	Pressure change of 3.6 to 6.0 mb
Rising / falling very rapidly	Pressure change of more than 6.0 mb
Now rising / falling	Pressure has been falling / rising or steady in the preceding 3 hours, but at the time of observation was definitely rising / falling

Inshore forecast:	**Sea state**
Smooth	Wave height less than 0.5 m
Slight	Wave height of 0.5 to 1.25 m
Moderate	Wave height of 1.25 to 2.5 m
Rough	Wave height of 2.5 to 4.0 m
Very rough	Wave height of 4.0 to 6.0 m
High	Wave height of 6.0 to 9.0 m
Very high	Wave height of 9.0 to 14.0 m
Phenomenal	Wave height more than 14.0 m

WEATHER MAPS

Weather maps for the UK generally cover most of NW Europe and the Atlantic and show the weather systems approaching from the west. They show the high and low pressure systems that give the varying conditions.

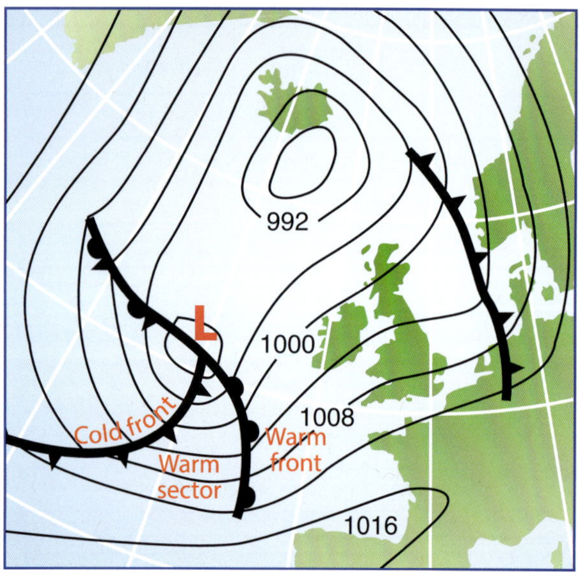

Low pressure systems

A low pressure system, also known as a depression, occurs when the weather is dominated by unstable conditions. In a depression air is rising, forming an area of low pressure at the surface. This rising air cools and condenses, encouraging cloud formation, so the weather is often cloudy and wet. Conditions are unsettled, often windy with major changes of wind direction. Visibility can be poor in the warm sector, especially in the spring, caused by advection or sea fog.

In the Northern Hemisphere winds blow in an anticlockwise direction around a depression (opposite in Southern Hemisphere) and the isobars are normally close together indicating strong winds. Low pressures bring fronts at the boundary between two different air masses, normally warm moist air from the tropics and cooler drier air from polar regions. A warm front is caused when a mass of warmed air overtakes and rises over a mass of cold air. Similarly a cold front is created when a mass of cold air pushes in under warm air. A front may sometimes be described in a forecast as a trough.

The wind blows almost parallel to the isobars, but angled inwards by about 10°, and the system tends to move in the direction of the isobars in the warm sector, between the two fronts. The cloud, rain and changes of wind direction occur on the fronts.

CLOUDS

Cirrus = feathery	Cirro = high	Nimbus = raining
Cumulus = heap	Alto = mid-height	Stratus = layer

Level	Name	Description
High level 11,000 m	Cirrus Cirrocumulus Cirrostratus	Mares tails Mackerel-like sky Halo around sun
Mid level 5,000 m	Altocumulus Altostratus Nimbostratus	Mackerel-like sky Featureless layer Raining
Low level 2,000 m	Stratocumulus Stratus	Rolls Featureless
Across all levels	Cumulonimbus Cumulus	Rain / thunder Cotton wool

Cirrus: Very high wispy clouds formed of ice crystals.

Cirrocumulus: Very high clouds that appear as small cumulus-type masses.

Cirrostratus: High sheets of thin ice cloud, often producing a halo effect around the sun or moon.

Altocumulus: Fairly high 'woolly' looking cloud.

Altostratus: Layer of almost unbroken cloud at medium height.

Nimbostratus: Low, heavy looking sheets of grey cloud, associated with continuous rain (e.g. at a warm front).

Stratocumulus: Cumulus clouds that have spread out and combined to form a broken sheet, or thin stratus that appears to be breaking up into separate clouds.

Stratus: Almost continuous sheets of low cloud; often grey and associated with drizzle.

Cumulonimbus: The classic 'thundercloud', with a fairly low cloud base but very high top (often flat).

Cumulus: Low, puffy clouds. Sometimes white and associated with fair weather but may grow upwards, produce showers and take on some of the characteristics of cumulonimbus.

WEATHER SYSTEMS

Passage of a depression

Observer is stationary in open water; the depression is moving quickly NE. The observer experiences A, B, C, D, E, F, G, H.

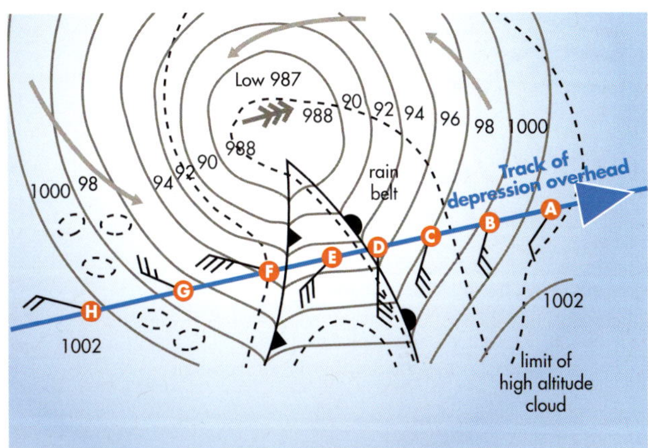

H	G	F	E	D	C	B	A	Pos'n
WxN4	NW5	WxN7/8	SW6	S7/8	SSW6	SxW5	SW2	**Wind**
1001	997	993	993	993	996	999	1001	**Baro**
None	Large Cumulus	Cumulo Nimbus	Stratus	Cloud	Lowering	Thickening	Cirrus & Cirro Stratus	**Cloud**
Fair	Showers	Rain/ Showers	Drizzle	Rain in last hr.	Continuous Mod. Rain	Fair	Fair	**Weather**
Swell from NW	Mod. NW	Rough W/SW/ NW	Mod. SW	Rough S&SW	Mod. SSW	Mod. SSW	Slight SW swell	**Sea State**
Good	Good	Poor	Mod. To Poor	Deterio-rates	Deterio-rates	Good	Good	**Visa-bility**

Progress of a depression

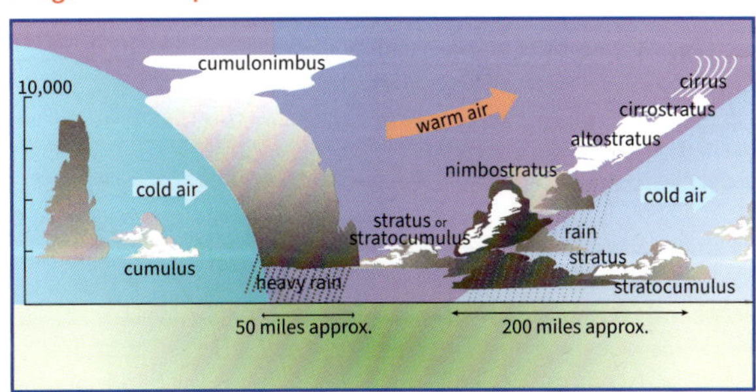

Buy Ballots Law

To track the progress of the low pressure past the boat's position Buy Ballot's law can be applied. This states that, in the Northern Hemisphere, if you stand with your back to the wind, the centre of the low will on your left hand side.

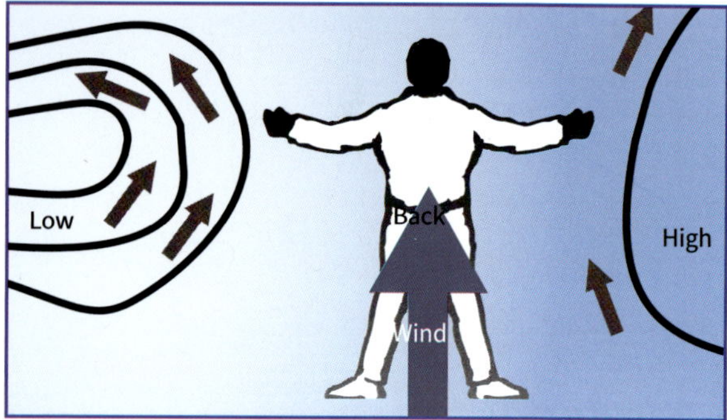

The opposite is true in the Southern Hemisphere.

High pressure systems

A high pressure system, or anticyclone, occurs when the weather is stable and air is descending, forming an area of higher pressure at the surface. With stable conditions, cloud formation is inhibited, so the weather is usually settled with little cloud. In spring, sea breezes may develop on the coast. Winds blow in a clockwise direction around an anticyclone, isobars are normally widely spaced and winds often quite light.

Winter anti-cyclones

In winter the clear, settled conditions and light winds can lead to frost and fog. The clear skies allow heat to be lost by radiation, leading to frost as temperatures fall overnight. Light winds and falling temperatures can cause fog to form. This is called **radiation** or **land fog**. It is common in estuaries but can also drift out to sea. This type of fog will generally burn off next day or be blown away if a wind develops.

Summer anti-cyclones

In summer the clear settled conditions can bring long sunny days and warm temperatures. The weather is normally dry, although occasionally very hot temperatures can trigger thunderstorms. After a few days poor visibility, known as high pressure haze, can develop as pollution is trapped by the descending air.

Advection or sea fog

Advection or sea fog is caused by warm moist air blowing in over cold water, and is common in the warm sector of a low pressure. In spring it is most common around the coast where the shallow water is very cold, but in summer and autumn sea fog is most frequently out to sea because the deep water has not warmed. This type of fog will not burn off or blow away, in fact the strong wind helps it form. It will disappear when there is a change of wind direction as the cold front passes.

LOCAL WINDS

Sea breeze & land breeze

A sea breeze blows from seaward towards the land and can be a significant feature along the coast in summer. It is caused by warm air rising over the land and air moving in from the sea to take its place. The sea breeze normally develops in the morning with a clear sky or light cloud, and by afternoon it may reach Force 4 or 5. It dies at sunset. As the day passes the direction of a sea breeze will veer, in the northern hemisphere, and may end up almost parallel to the coast.

Sea breeze mechanism

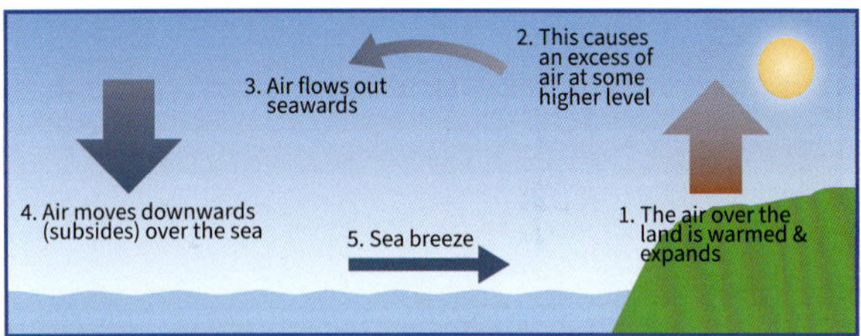

Land breeze

The opposite effect at night causes a land breeze. The wind blows seawards from the land. Land breezes occur in clear weather at night or in the early morning as the land cools, and the air above it is cooled, becomes denser and 'drains' out to sea down valleys.

The effect may extend only a couple of miles out to sea, and the strength depends on the contours of the land. Where the coastline is very steep the breeze will be stronger and is known an a katabatic wind.

Turbulence & gusts

Close to the shore and in rivers the winds can be fluky as headlands cause turbulence and gusts blow from valleys and behind trees.

Coastal winds

Whenever the wind blows over the surface of the earth, drag reduces the speed of the surface wind to less than the wind at several hundred feet. At sea surface wind is angled about 10° to 20° anticlockwise (in the Northern Hemisphere – opposite in the Southern Hemisphere) from the higher altitude wind. Over land there is more drag and the surface wind is angled about 20° to 40°.

Where the wind is blowing generally offshore or onshore this change of wind direction is gradual.

Convergence & divergence

Where the wind is blowing along the coast, the difference in wind direction has a different effect.

Convergence

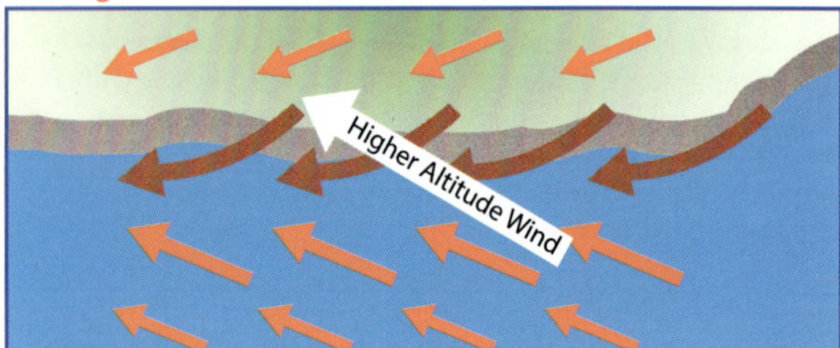

Divergence

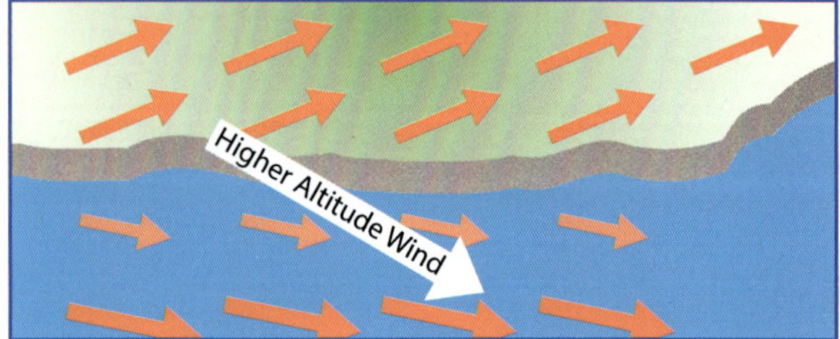

If the land is to the left when you are standing with your back to the wind, the winds over the land and sea will be diverging, so the coastal wind will be lighter than the offshore wind.

(Buy Ballots law means the centre of the low is on left.)

If the land is on your right when you are standing with your back to the wind, the winds over the land and sea will be converging creating a funnelling effect and stronger winds along the coast.

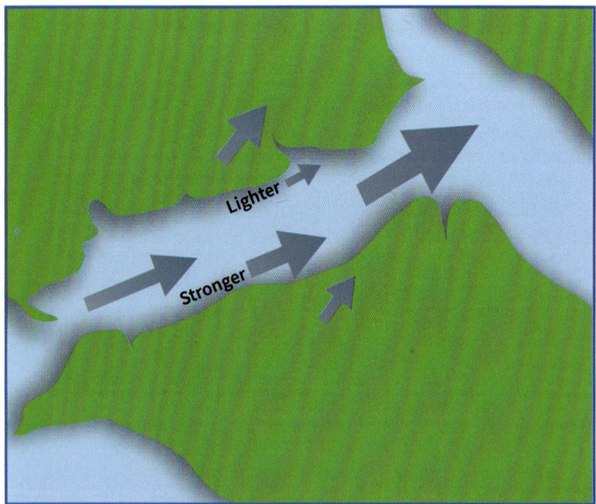

UK SEA AREAS

SE
Iceland
Faeroes
Fair
Isle
Viking
N Ulsire
Bailey
Hebrides
Cromarty
Forties
S Ulsire
Fisher
Rockall
Malin
Forth
Dogger
German
Bight
Tyne
Humber
Shannon
Thames
Fastnet
Dover
Sole
Wight
Portland
Plymouth
FitzRoy
Biscay
Trafalgar

PART 6.
FLAGS

A Alpha
• –
B Bravo
– • • •
C Charlie
– • – •
D Delta
– • •
E Echo
•
F Foxtrot
• • – •
G Golf
– – •
H Hotel
• • • •
I India
• •
J Juliet
• – – –
K Kilo
– • –
L Lima
• – • •
M Mike
– –
N November
– •
O Oscar
– – –
P Papa
• – – •
Q Quebec
– – • –
R Romeo
• – •
S Sierra
• • •
T Tango
–
U Uniform
• • –
V Victor
• • • –
W Whisky
• – –
X X-ray
– • • –
Y Yankee
– • – –
Z Zulu
– – • •
Code and answering pennant

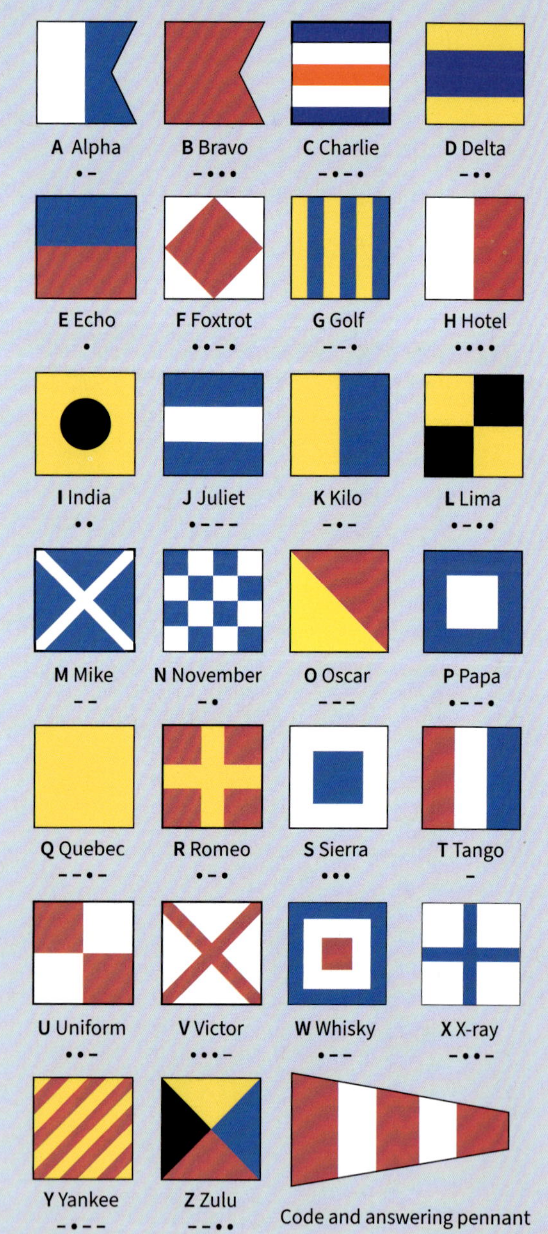

NUMERAL PENNANTS & SUBSTITUTES

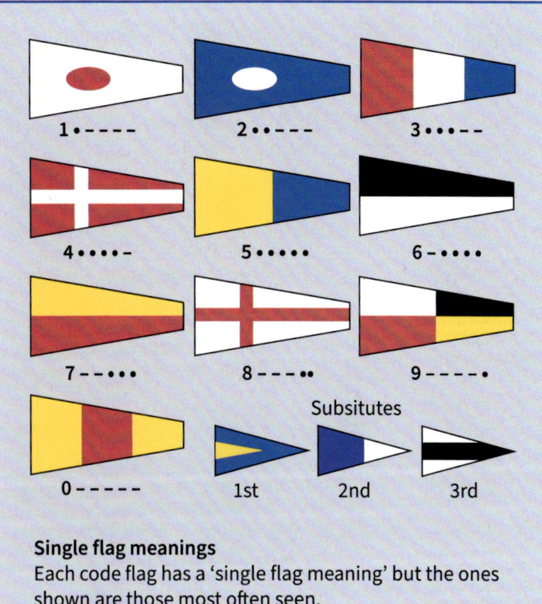

Single flag meanings
Each code flag has a 'single flag meaning' but the ones shown are those most often seen.

A I have a diver down: keep clear at low speed.

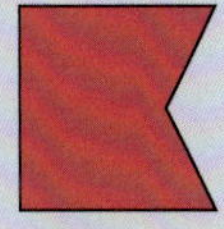

B I am taking in or discharging dangerous goods. (Usually flown by tankers.)

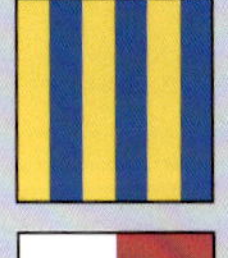

G I require a pilot.

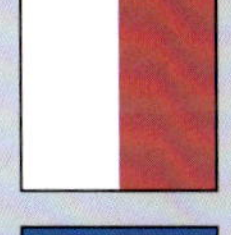

H I have a pilot on board.

P My vessel is about to proceed to sea.

Q My vessel is healthy and I require free pratique and customs clearance.

PART 7.
SEAMANSHIP

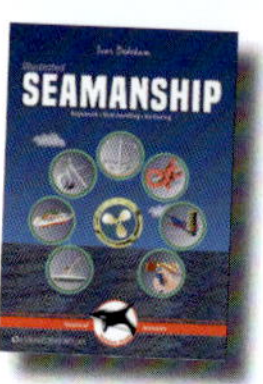

Seamanship skills are devloped with practice, but the key elements are covered here. A much fuller coverage can be found in *Illustrated Seamanship*.

ANCHORING

Most boats carry a 10 kg to 15 kg anchor, with 8 mm chain, depending on the boat's length and weight. The recommendation will vary with the type of anchor:

- Chain is preferable to warp.
- Have at least 5 m of chain between warp and anchor if not using all chain. This prevents chafe, and allows a more horizontal pull on the anchor.
- Anchor warp should be nylon, to give some stretch.
- Do not stow other items, such as fenders, on top of the anchor and chain in case the anchor is needed in a hurry.
- Carry a kedge anchor in addition to the main anchor.
- Put out at least 4 x depth for chain and 6 x depth for warp in calm conditions, and more if rough.

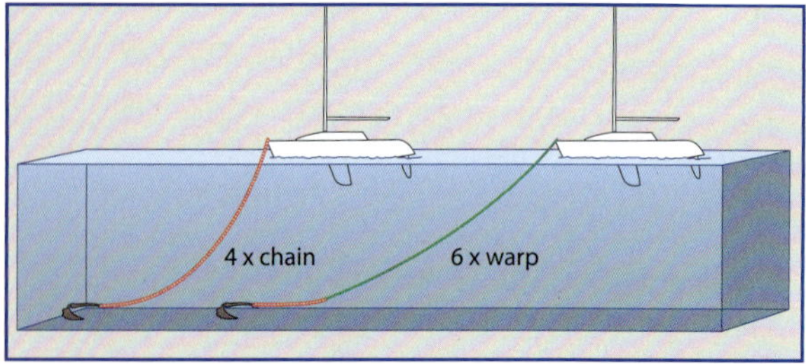

Anchor gear

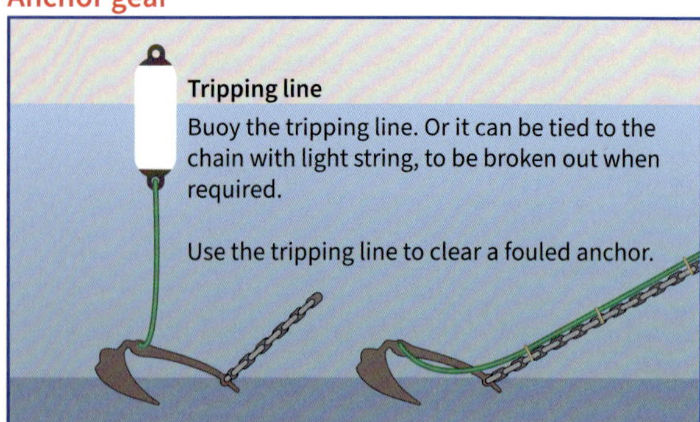

- Mouse the anchor shackle so it can't come undone.
- Mark the chain and warp to show how much has been let go.
- Secure the inboard end in the anchor locker – in such a way that it can be cut.

Where to anchor

- Good holding ground.
- Consult the pilot book.
- Good shelter from wind, including any changes forecast.
- Clear of a strong tidal stream.
- Adequate room to swing. A yacht will almost always lie to the tidal stream, but a motor cruiser is more influenced by wind direction, so they will not swing at the same time.
- Sufficient depth of water.
- Out of busy channels and areas of moorings.

How to anchor

- Flake the required length of chain and warp on deck.
- Prepare the anchor for letting go.
- Under engine, approach into the tidal stream.
- Under sail, approach into the tidal stream under sail or sails that can be let fly and allow the boat to stop.
- Stop, then let go the anchor as the boat drifts backwards.
- Motor astern to dig it in fully, if necessary.
- Take a transit or bearings to check for dragging.
- Secure the anchor cable to cleat.
- After anchoring use a retaining pin over the chain so it cannot jump out of the bow roller.
- Put up the anchor ball or show an anchor light at night.
- If the anchor is fouled, you may be able to motor over it, taking in the slack, and break it out.

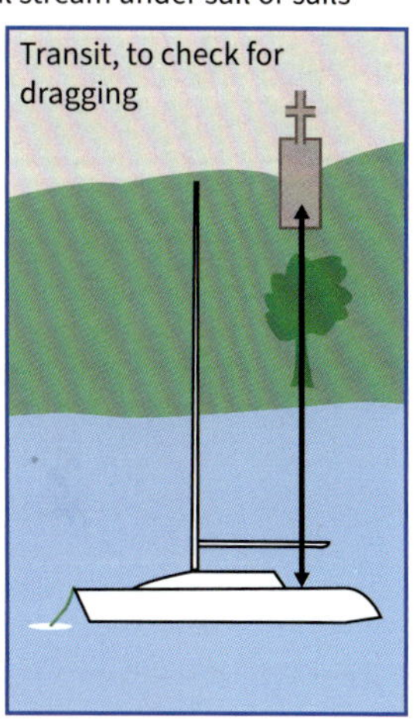
Transit, to check for dragging

Anchor snagged on a cable

- If a cable is snagged, pull up the anchor.
- Slip a rope around the cable, and make fast.
- Drop the anchor until clear, and then retrieve it.
- Finally, release the cable.

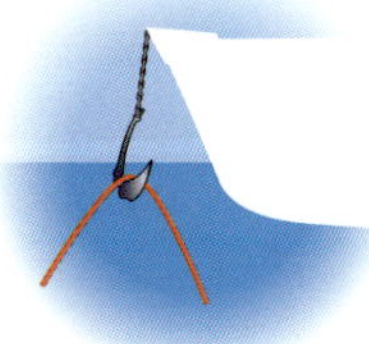

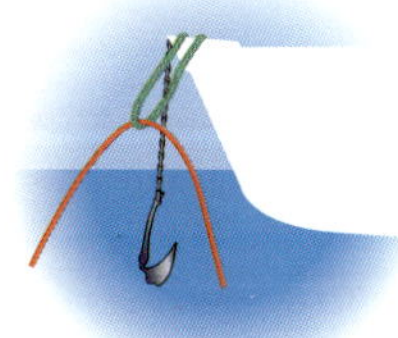

Using two anchors

The Fork Moor is useful for added security, especially in very strong winds. It also reduces yawing.

1. Drop first anchor. If one anchor is warp and chain, use that first.
2. Motor to where second anchor is to be dropped, and let it go. A line drawn between the anchors should be at right angles to direction of wind. This is easier to judge if first anchor is buoyed.
3. Drop back, while adjusting both, so that strain is equal. Angle should be about 45°.

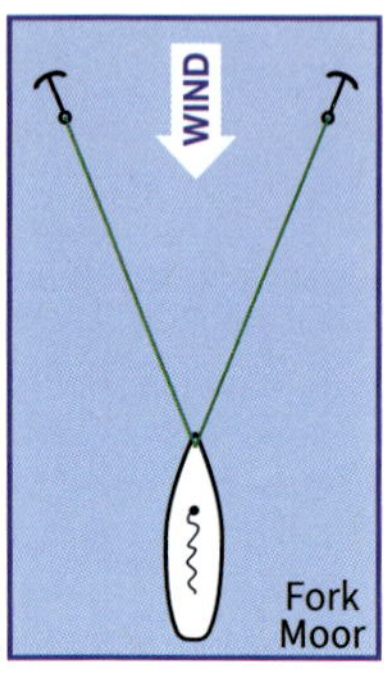

The Bahamian Moor is useful to reduce swinging room in a crowded anchorage, and in an area where a tide flows through the anchorage.

1. Drop the main anchor first. Go astern, paying out twice the normal amount of cable.
2. Let go the second anchor. Pay out its cable while heaving in on the first anchor until the boat is centred.

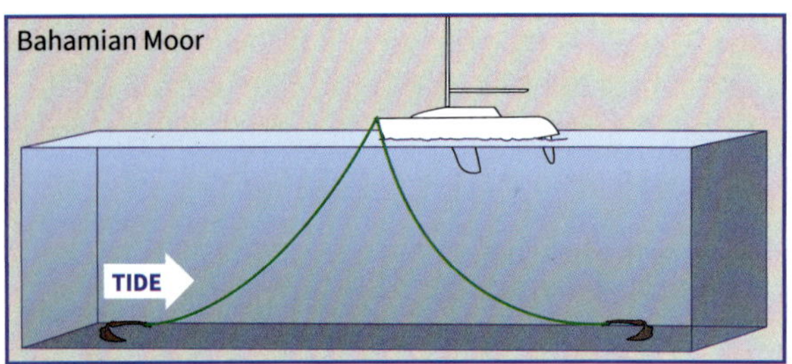

ENTERING A MARINA OR LOCK

- Contact the marina for a berth, VHF is usually best.
- Prepare the boat with fenders and bow and stern lines on both sides even for your own berth with fixed lines.
- Brief the crew to keep a good lookout for other craft and what to do once ashore.
- Have a boathook ready if entering a lock.
- Consider how the wind will affect the boat, and if there will be any tidal stream.

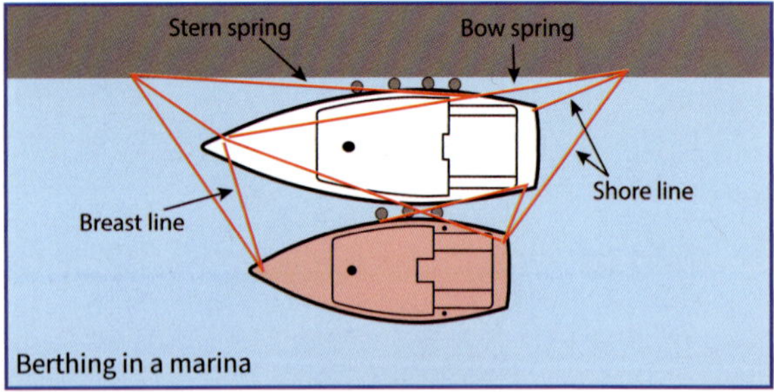

After berthing:

- Secure the boat with seperate lines, taking all spare rope onboard.
- Check fender heights.
- Tidy sails and deck.
- Switch off instruments, navigation light and VHF cockpit speaker.
- Connect shore power.

MOORING ON A BUOY

- Choose a suitable mooring for the boat, consider size, shelter.
- Check there is sufficient depth of water for duration of the stay.
- Check the availability, if possible.
- Prepare warps and boathook and brief the crew which side it will be.
- Approach as the other boats are lying, usually into the tidal stream in the case of a yacht.

KNOTS

Round turn & two half hitches: Attaching a rope to a post.

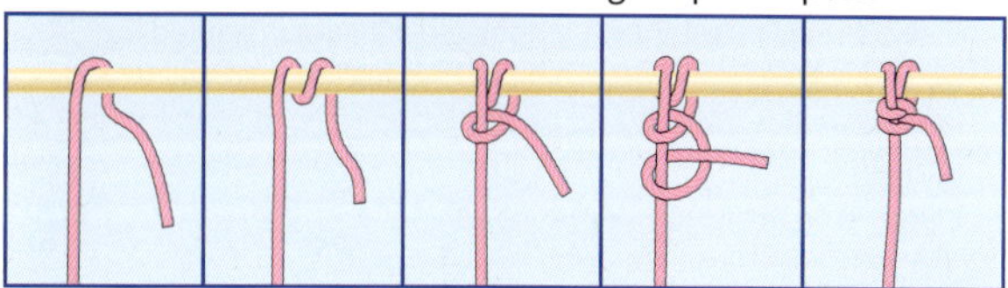

Clove hitch: Attaching a rope to a ring or post.

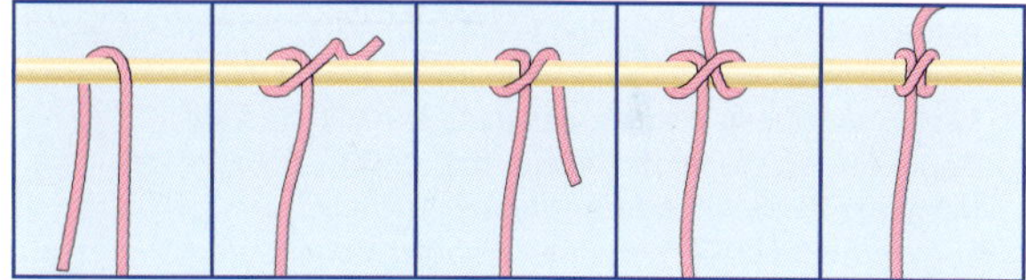

Sheet bend: Joining two ropes of similar thickness.

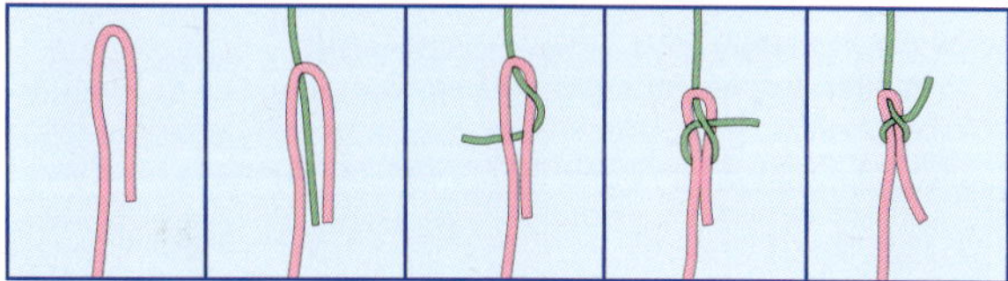

Bowline: Making a secure loop in a rope.

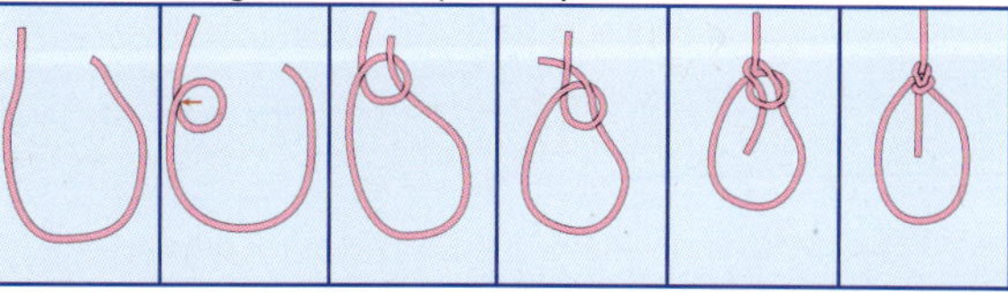

PART 8. MAINTENANCE & TROUBLESHOOTING

LOOKING AFTER THE HULL

Seacocks

- Seacocks must move freely. If stiff, strip and refit when the boat is hauled out.
- There should be no corrosion, and make sure each pipe is secured with two stainless steel hose clips.
- Have a softwood bung next to each seacock.
- Cockpit drains should be fitted with seacocks too.

Steering gear

- Inspect rudder fastenings whenever the boat is hauled out.
- Rods or cables joining a wheel to the rudder head will usually be concealed; they should be inspected for wear and lubricated annually.
- Inspect the steering quadrant's stops inside the hull. If worn, the quadrant may ride over them and jam.
- Try out the emergency tiller fitting.

Hauling out

- **Water intakes** for toilets and engines may have strainers, which must be clean and clear.
- Renew **sacrificial zinc anodes** that are badly wasted.
- **Depth finder:** Clean off the external transducer in the hull. Normally this will not be antifouled.
- **Log / speedometer:** Withdraw any retractable fittings and clean, being careful to avoid damage.
- **Rudder fittings:** Inspect carefully and check for excessive play.
- **Stern gland and shaft bearing:** If gland has been leaking re-packing or replacement may be necessary.
- **Propeller:** Inspect for signs of damage.

If necessary seek professional advice with these checks.

CHECKLIST: LAYING UP

Checklist for end of season

General

- ☐ **Diesel tank:** Fill to reduce chance of condensation.
- ☐ Set up **dehumidifier** or heating on the boat if possible.
- ☐ **Portable valuables:** Remove binoculars, portable radios, etc., unless they are quite secure on board.
- ☐ Remove **gear** from the boat that may get damp.
- ☐ **Water tanks:** Empty. Before next season flush through with specialist cleaning product.
- ☐ **Toilets:** Flush through thoroughly, then close seacocks & winterise according to maker's instructions. Stripping & refitting is usually advised.

Mast & standing rigging

Mast: If it is to be unstepped:

- ☐ **Electrical leads:** Tallied to ensure easy reconnecting.
- ☐ **Standing rigging:** Labelled before taking off mast.
- ☐ **Mast & spars:** Marked with boat's name before stowing ashore.

Electrical

- ☐ **Batteries:** Unless they are to be kept on charge aboard, remove ashore for care.
- ☐ **Dry batteries:** Remove from torches, radios, lifebelt lights & any other equipment.
- ☐ Spray battery connections with WD40 or similar.

Sails & running rigging

- ☐ **Sails:** Send to sailmaker for repairs and / or laundry.
- ☐ **Running rigging:** Un-reeve, check for wear, label & stow.
- ☐ **Self-furling gear:** Un-rig & follow maker's instructions for seasonal maintenance.

Engine

- ☐ Close sea water intake, having made sure that the engine cannot be started. If needed, flush cooling water system with fresh water, drain & winterise according to maker's instructions.
- ☐ Check recommended maintenance schedule. Regardless of hours run it is sensible to change engine oil & filter & fuel filters during lay-up.

Safety equipment

- ☐ **Liferaft:** Send for servicing if needed.
- ☐ **Lifejackets:** Inspect & service.
- ☐ **Flares:** Check for expiry date.
- ☐ **First aid kit:** Remove for checking.
- ☐ **Jackstays:** Remove to prevent deterioration & inspect for wear.

Domestic

- ☐ **Food:** Remove ALL food, including dry provisions & canned goods.
- ☐ **Cool box or fridge:** Empty, clean & leave open.
- ☐ **Toilet & shower compartment:** Clean with sanitiser to reduce mildew.
- ☐ **Sleeping bags & towels:** Remove for washing.
- ☐ **Waterproofs:** Remove to wash.

CHECKLIST: FITTING OUT

Final checklist for beginning of the season

- ☐ Insurance policy in place
- ☐ All gear back on board
- ☐ Bilges clean & pumps tested
- ☐ Charts & almanac updated
- ☐ Fill fresh water tanks, pumps tested for leaks
- ☐ All safety equipment serviced & back in place
- ☐ Navigation lights & instruments checked
- ☐ Engine de-winterised
- ☐ Impellor & filter checked or replaced as necessary
- ☐ Sails, halyards & sheets all running correctly
- ☐ Flares in date
- ☐ Compass light & navigation lights working
- ☐ Seacocks all moving freely
- ☐ Steering gear checked for leaks
- ☐ Battery charging & holding its charge
- ☐ Gas system checked
- ☐ All battery-operated equipment working
- ☐ Guardrail condition & tension checked
- ☐ Jackstays replaced

Download from www.fernhurstbooks.com, search for Skipper's Pocketbook and click on 'Additional Rescources'

ENGINE

Engine failure is the most common cause of Coastguard incidents and lifeboat callouts, sometimes for vessels which have merely run out of fuel!

The clear aims for a skipper:

1. Prevent breakdowns by regular engine maintenance, and engine checks before every sail.
2. Having the ability to deal with a minor breakdown at sea.

It is essential to be able to identify the key parts on the engine.

A Oil filler
B Oil filter
C Seawater pump
D Fuel filter (fine filter)
E Fuel feed pump
F Engine oil dipstick
G Fuel injection pump
H Regulator handle
I Engine stop lever

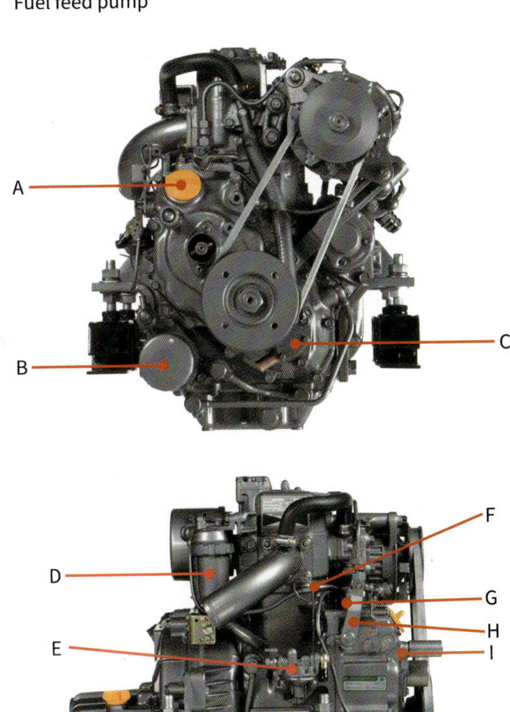

A clean engine compartment makes it much easier to spot corrosion, leaks or other defects.

CHECKLIST: PRE-SAIL ENGINE CHECKS

The engine manual will advise, but this is a useful guide:

Fuel

- ☐ Check fuel levels & spare can is full.
- ☐ Use fuel treatment regularly to absorb water from fuel, if necessary, & prevent the growth of diesel bug.

Engine

- ☐ **Engine compartment:** Open & look around. Look for oil or water leaks, or loose wires.
- ☐ **Belts:** Check they are sound & tight.
- ☐ **Seawater inlet valve:** Check it is open & the strainer clear.
- ☐ **Oil level:** Check with the dipstick, but do not overfill.
- ☐ **Header tank:** Check the fresh water level.
- ☐ **Fuel pre-filter:** Check & drain any water.
- ☐ Put the gearbox in neutral, start the engine, & run it at medium revs to warm it up.
- ☐ Check the ahead / astern operation, cooling water discharge, oil pressure & that batteries are charging.
- ☐ **Stern gland:** Check this periodically for leaks while the engine is running. Tighten the grease filler, if there is one, as required.
- ☐ **Anodes:** Check on a regular basis - as often as every two months if the boat is kept in the water.

Gearbox

- ☐ **Oil:** Check weekly when the engine is running & is warm.

At sea

- ☐ Keep an eye on the instruments that monitor oil pressure, temperature & battery charging.
- ☐ Check inside the engine compartment occasionally for signs of a leak.

Download from www.fernhurstbooks.com, search for Skipper's Pocketbook and click on 'Additional Rescources'

Troubleshooting & repairs

Engine will not start

PROBLEM 1: Starter motor will not turn or turns too slowly to start engine.

1. Check battery with voltmeter.
   - Try other battery – or both batteries together.
   - Try starting with decompression lever engaged, closing it when the engine is turning OK.
2. Check that connections to the battery terminals are clean and tight.
3. Check there are no loose wiring connections to starter motor, starter switch, and battery selection switch.

One fully charged battery must always be kept for starting, which is the most important job a battery has to do.

PROBLEM 2: Starter motor turns engine, but engine will not start. Take care not to run the battery flat.

1. Check there is fuel in the tank and the fuel isolation switch is open.
   NOTE: If fuel tank is ever refilled after being empty, it may be necessary to bleed fuel system.
2. Check engine stop valve is not open. Cable operated valves may stick, and electrically operated valves may jam in the closed position.
3. There may be air in the fuel. This is the most likely cause of non-starting. Check for loose connections in fuel lines.
4. Bleed fuel system.

Do not turn the engine over for more than 15 seconds without closing the cooling water inlet. Otherwise water may be sucked into the cylinder, destroying the engine. If it does fire, quickly open the inlet.

Bleeding the fuel system

This operation is needed to remove air from the fuel system. Bleeding is also required after changing fuel filters, after any other work on the fuel system and after running out of fuel.

The 'bleeding points' may vary and will be shown in the engine manual.

1. Identify the bleed screw and slacken it off. Normally this is on the fine filter housing (A).
2. Work the hand priming lever on the fuel lift pump (B).
3. If the fuel coming from the vent contains bubbles it is a sign of air in the system. Continue pumping until clear fuel flows out with no bubbles. Then tighten the screw while continuing to

operate the lift pump.

4. If no fuel comes from the vent, the primary fuel filter (between the fuel tank and engine) may be blocked. Close the fuel cut-off at the tank, clean out the filter, replace the element and turn the fuel back on before completing the bleeding process.
5. If, after replacing the primary fuel filter, the fuel still does not flow: Replace the element in fine filter and repeat operation.
6. If clear fuel comes from vent but, after tightening the vent, the engine still does not start: Slacken the high pressure line to one injector, turn over engine until fuel flows without bubbles, and then re-tighten.

In practice, bleeding the fuel system is usually successful after step 3.

Remember: There are two basic requirements:

1. Fuel must clearly be able to pass through both filters.
2. The fuel system must be completely free of air.

Engine overheating

Many engines have an alarm that sounds if the engine overheats. Further evidence will be the temperature gauge on the instrument panel, and no cooling water flowing from the exhaust. Overheating will not stop an engine from starting or running but will rapidly cause engine damage.

1. Stop the engine.
2. Check seawater intake is clear:
   - Close seacock on intake.
   - Open filter and remove any debris.

   Plastic bags can block water intakes, but may float free when the engine is stopped.
3. Check the seawater pump for impellor damage. An indication is that the cover plate on the pump is hot.
4. To check:
   - Close the inlet seacock.
   - Unscrew the pump cover plate.
   - Remove the damaged impellor.
   - Remove any debris from the system in the pump inlet and outlet.
   - Wipe over the blade of the new impellor with vaseline or similar, as this helps installation.
   - Insert new impellor using a clockwise rotating movement and replace the cover plate.

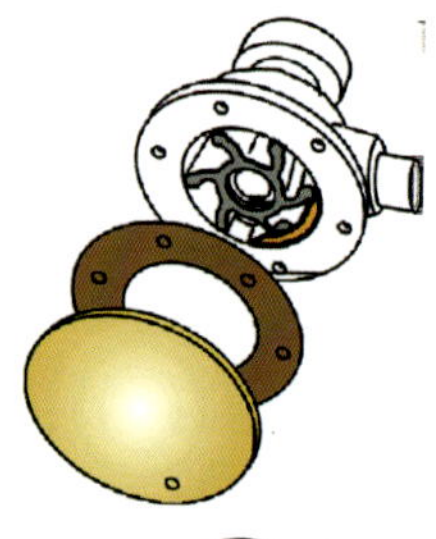

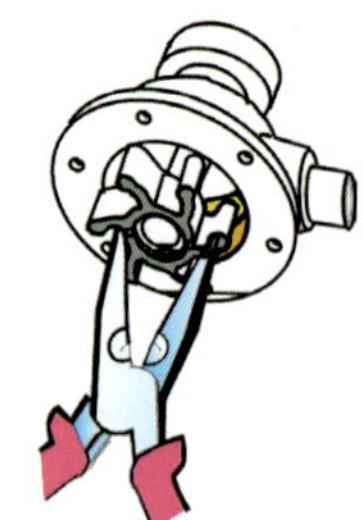

CHECKLIST: TOOLS & SPARES

- ☐ Set of spanners / wrenches – imperial and / or metric as required. Combined open ended / ring spanners are best, preferably with slim jaws to ease access to difficult nuts & bolts.
- ☐ Adjustable spanners – 3 sizes
- ☐ Mole grips
- ☐ Electrical wire strippers
- ☐ Crosshead screwdrivers
- ☐ Midget screwdriver for electrical work
- ☐ Right-angled screwdrivers
- ☐ Needle-nosed pliers
- ☐ Cold chisel
- ☐ Hacksaw & blades
- ☐ Hand drill & drill set
- ☐ Socket set for engine work
- ☐ Spanner to fit the stern gland
- ☐ Strap wrench for undoing filters
- ☐ 'Allen' hexagonal key set
- ☐ Slip joint pliers
- ☐ Screwdrivers – 3 sizes
- ☐ Stub screwdriver
- ☐ Electrical pliers
- ☐ Hammer
- ☐ Punch
- ☐ Files – round & flat

Engine spares
Also consult handbook or local agent.

- ☐ Water pump impellors & gaskets
- ☐ An element for fuel pre-filter
- ☐ A fuel fine filter element
- ☐ Sufficient lubricating oil to refill engine
- ☐ Fuel lift pump repair kit or complete replacement pump
- ☐ Spare belts for water pump & alternator

There are different types and sizes of engine spare, such as belts & impellors, that look similar. When ordering spares it is important to quote the serial number.

General maintenance gear

- ☐ Selection of hose clamps
- ☐ Plastic tubing in various sizes
- ☐ Self-amalgamating repair tape
- ☐ Electrical tape
- ☐ Selection of electrical terminals
- ☐ WD40 or similar
- ☐ Petroleum jelly
- ☐ Stern tube packing in the correct size, if required

Download from www.fernhurstbooks.com, search for Skipper's Pocketbook and click on 'Additional Rescources'

PART 9.
SKIPPERING

GENERAL ORGANISATION

- Ensure crew have warm and effective waterproof clothing, non-slip shoes and boots. Thermal wicking materials that will breath are best under waterproof clothing. Avoid cotton which will tend to hold moisture and sweat, and make people feel cold. Polarised sunglasses, caps and sun cream are all important too.
- Check with everyone if they have any medical condition that is likely to affect them during the passage, and a supply of medication if required. Ask for details of care that they might need if they become unwell. This should include seasickness.
- Suitable and convenient meals need to be planned and prepared, also snacks and hot drinks need to be easily available. On a long passage meals will need to be planned to fit the watch keeping system. Food is important for energy and crew morale and simple food can be prepared in advance. A well-designed and organised galley should be usable even in poor weather.
- In marinas noise can be a major aggravation to others, so turn off external speakers, avoid loud music, flapping halyards and general disturbance from crew returning from a night ashore or leaving before dawn on a passage or race.
- Be considerate of other boats when moored alongside by always crossing quietly, via the foredeck, being prepared to move quickly if the inner boat wants to leave, running shorelines and taking care that spreaders cannot clash if there is any wash.

WATCHES & NIGHT PASSAGES

Normally a system of watches should be set up for a night passage, and for a long day passage too. Watches should be started soon after leaving harbour, otherwise all the crew become tired at the same time. Getting overtired, cold, hungry and dehydrated can have very serious consequences.

- The skipper must consider carefully at what stages in the passage they can rest, and so be available and alert for crossing shipping lanes, making landfall and entering a harbour.
- The best arrangement and the length of watches must depend on the number and strength of the crew, and on the weather. Longer watches allow more sleep for those off watch but, in bad weather and on a short passage, shorter watches may be better.
- Ideally no crew will be on watch alone at night, near land or in crowded waters.

Two Watches	A	2000 - 2300
	B	2300 - 0200
	A	0200 - 0500
Three Watches	A	2000 - 2200
	B	2200 - 2400
	C	2400 - 0200

STANDING ORDERS

Skippers might also consider having standing orders, or setting night orders, especially on longer passages. These might include:

- Using safety harnesses at night or when the boat is reefed.
- Situations when the skipper should be woken, such as if an alteration of course is necessary, a reef is required, a vessel is within a set range or at any time when crew are concerned.
- A watch on deck should be maintained at all times. If it is necessary to go below for longer than a few seconds extra help should be called.
- Lifejackets always to be worn, unless the skipper has decided that it is safe not to, and always in the dinghy.
- Saloon and galley lights not to be used at night but only red or other lights which do not damage the night vision of watch keepers on deck.
- The MOB equipment and liferaft must be ready for immediate use at sea. Any harbour security lashing should be removed before sailing.
- Hatches should be closed at sea.
- Having clear rules about the use of gas.
- Having a policy on the use of alcohol and smoking .

DOCUMENTS & REGULATIONS

Some regulations apply at all times to all vessels:

- Complying with the Collision Regulations.
- Rendering assistance to a vessel in distress, if possible and safe to do so.
- Reporting distress signals and hazards to the Coastguard.
- Not using distress signals unless in distress.
- Carrying a radar reflector.
- Having on board a copy of the Lifesaving Signals.
- Making a passage plan.
- Additional local rules set by local Ports, Harbour or River Authorities.

Many of these rules are covered in Chapter V of the Safety of Life at Sea Convention (SOLAS).

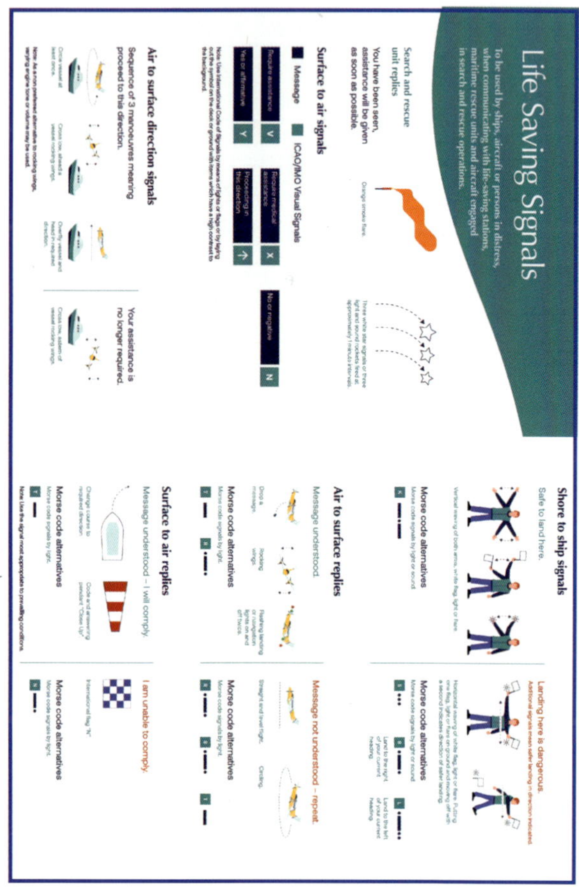

This table contains public sector information licensed under the Open Government Licence v1.0

When sailing outside the waters of their own home country, boats have the right of passage through the territorial waters of another country, but cruising and visiting ports overseas brings them under the jurisdiction of the Coastal State as well. The Coastal State's rules and regulations then apply in addition to those of their Flag State.

These conditions are set out in the United Nations Convention on the Law of the Sea (UNCLOS).

Additional documentation

Required for a private vessel in the UK:

- Ship's Radio Licence

Recommended in the UK:

- Insurance
- Using the RYA SafeTrx App

Additional requirements and regulations for the boat when overseas may include:

- Flying the Flag State maritime ensign
- As a courtesy, flying the national maritime flag of the Coastal State at the starboard crosstrees
- Holding tanks
- Documents:
  - Registration document
  - Bill of sale
  - Evidence of VAT paid
  - Evidence of RCD compliance after 1998 on the CE plate
  - Receipts to show red diesel bought tax-paid in the UK
  - Notice of variation to ship's radio licence to show ATIS-enabled radio

Requirements for the skipper and / or crew in the UK:

- Radio certificate

A crew member without a radio certificate may use the radio under the close supervision of a qualified operator.

Additional requirements and regulations for the skipper and / or crew overseas may include:

- Certificate of competency, such as an International Certificate of Competency
- Passport
- UK Global Health Insurance card

On vessels used commercially and private leisure vessels over 13.7m there are regulations that apply even in the UK. These include qualification, equipment and documentation. Overseas there are different regulations that vary from country to country.

To get up to date information for specific counties the RYA website (**www.rya.org.uk**) is excellent.

Ship's radio licence

A radio licence from OFCOM is required for the boat and must list all the transmitting radio equipment on board. This includes the VHF/DCS set, portable radio, radar, EPIRB, SART, PLB and AIS if it transmits. The licence must be renewed every 10 years, or when details change. Obtaining the licence through the OFCOM website (**www.ofcom.org.uk**) is free. The licence will provide the MMSI and International call-sign for the radio.

It may be necessary to comply with the RAINWAT or Regional Arrangement Concerning the Radiotelephone Service on Inland

Waterways regulations if the boat will enter the inland waterways of many European counties. These regulations require the radio to operate in ATIS or Automatic Transmitter Identification System mode which identifies vessels by their radio transmissions. An ATIS number and Notice of Variation (NoV) to the ship's radio licence from OFCOM will be required, as well as a radio that is ATIS enabled. Some sets allow the user to switch between ATIS and non-ATIS use. Consult the instruction manual or ask a dealer. ATIS is not used in the UK and should be deselected before making the return passage.

An Active Radar Target Enhancer will also require a NoV.

ICC or International Certificate of Competence

A skipper of a private leisure vessel in the UK does not require a licence or evidence of competence.

This is not always true in other countries. Requirements vary from country to country, and it is important to check. The ICC is the most widely recognised certificate overseas, but there is no guarantee that it will be accepted.

The application form explains that the ICC can be achieved by an assessment at an RYA Training Centre or some Affiliated Clubs or by using other certificates as evidence. The form can be found on the RYA website: www.rya.org.uk/knowledge/abroad/icc/icc-apply.

Registration

A yacht used solely in British waters does not have to be registered but, when cruising abroad, registration on the Small Ships Register is required. Most boats can be on SRR – Part III and it is easy and inexpensive to organise. The SSR number must then be displayed.

Customs & entry requirements

It may be necessary to enter a country at a specify port of entry and, if from a different customs area, fly the Q flag until given clearance from the authorities. Until that time the crew should remain on board. Requirements may depend on the port of departure and nationality of all on board.

The crew may have passport checks and be expected to clear immigration in some counties.

Check for country-specific and up to date information before overseas passages.

Customs Notice 8 explains the customs requirements for private individuals who sail their pleasure craft to and from the UK. It includes customs procedures for arriving and departing the UK and details on temporary importation for pleasure craft registered outside the EU.

INDEX